Walks From Colwyn Bay

Christopher Draper

Carreg Gwalch

ISBN: 0-86381-604-5

Cover design: Alan Jones

First published in 2000 by
Gwasg Carreg Gwalch, 12 Iard yr Orsaf, Llanrwst, Wales LL26 0EH
☎ 01492 642031   🖷 01492 641502
✆ books@carreg-gwalch.co.uk   Web site: www.carreg-gwalch.co.uk

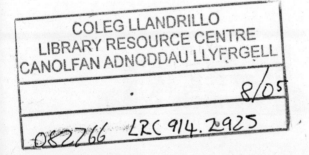

For Rebecca's daughters

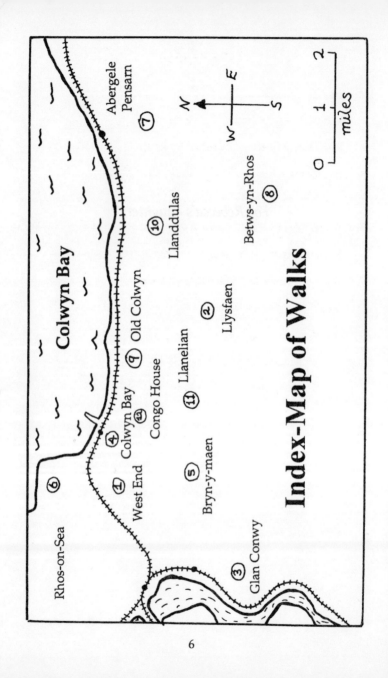

Index-Map of Walks

Colwyn Bay

Rhos-on-Sea

Abergele Pensarm ⑦

Llanddulas ⑩

Betws-yn-Rhos ⑧

Old Colwyn ⑨

Llysfaen ②

Colwyn Bay ⑫
Congo House

Llanelian ⑪

West End ①

④

⑥

Bryn-y-maen ⑤

Glan Conwy ③

N
W — E
S

0   1   2
miles

6

Contents

Introduction

Every feature of our towns and countryside has a history. A hedge may define a field created by a nineteenth century enclosure; a footpath might connect two long-abandoned farms; a bus stop can mark a route created by a long-dead transport pioneer; and a hardware shop may once have been a palace of dreams. Castles and cathedrals are well known and protected but much of our everyday social history is neglected and forgotten. I have tried to piece together interesting stories, events and lives from the area around Colwyn Bay; not always grand, but invariably fascinating. Some walks create a narrative as their particular story unfolds, other walks provide a general introduction to a small village or part of the town itself.

Although Colwyn Bay is the largest settlement on the north coast of Wales it is also one of the youngest. Your explorations will take you beyond the town limits to some of the older, rural communities, from Llansanffraid Glan Conwy in the west to Abergele in the east, and south to Llanfair Talhaearn. Taken together these twelve walks will provide an introduction and insight into the history of Colwyn Bay and its hinterland.

Each route has been composed to maximise both interest and enjoyment, and minimise mileage and endurance. Any moderately fit person should have no trouble completing all twelve walks. No walk would take more than three hours to race around, but I would recommend allowing an average of four or five hours for a more civilised, informative experience and even longer if you include a leisurely lunch. No special equipment is necessary but it's always wise to carry a waterproof jacket. Stout shoes or boots are a good idea and wearing shorts is a bad idea, unless you enjoy the gentle caress of nettles and thorns. Route finding shouldn't be a problem as each walk includes detailed directions and identifies numerous reference points along the way, but an Ordnance Survey map will provide a useful overall plan of the area. Landranger map

116 covers all walks except for number three, which continues onto Landranger 115. Some people might find the book of local maps published by 'Streetwise' (ISBN 1-898599-65-3) an easier to follow, and cheaper, option.

The practical details are set out at the beginning of each chapter and, where a particular walk doesn't start from the centre of Colwyn Bay, I have given public transport details. These local bus and train routes are as much a part of the history of the area as the footpaths, farms and churchyards and by using them, rather than private transport, you help preserve and enhance the environment that you seek to explore. Simply by walking these local footpaths you are helping maintain our precious ancient rights of access to the countryside and to our shared history, and you get a nice day out too!

Happy walking.

Christopher Draper

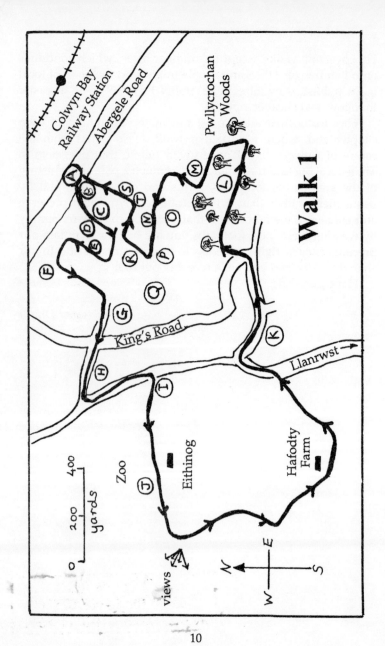

Walk 1

Colwyn Bay Railway Station

Abergele Road

Pwllycrochan Woods

King's Road

Llanrwst →

Zoo

Eithinog

Hafodty Farm

views

N
W E
S

yards
0   200   400

A B C D E F G H I J K L M N O P Q R S T

Where Leafy Splendour Reigns

Walk Number:	One
Distance:	Four miles
Terrain:	Some moderate ascents and descents with paved, field and wooded sections
Start:	War Memorial in Queen's Gardens
Finish:	Circular route
Transport:	Centrally located
Refreshments:	Taylor's Restaurant, Wentworth Avenue

Introduction:

At the beginning of the nineteenth century Conwy was a town, Llandudno was a village and Colwyn Bay didn't exist. The town really began with the sale of the Pwllycrochan Estate in 1865. The main purchaser was a Manchester manufacturer whose agent, John Porter, converted the old Pwllycrochan mansion into an hotel and began promoting the area under the anglophilic name of Colwyn Bay. As well attracting tourists the aim was to provide residences for wealthy businessmen, both active and retired, from the booming industrial areas of the north-west of England. The town planning was less extensive and less consistent than that achieved in Llandudno but in the early stages, at least, a very pleasant and attractive residential environment was created. Commodious villas were laid out along elegant tree-lined avenues and over the years much of their character and ambience has been retained. This walk explores an area which extends up the tree-clad slopes to Upper Colwyn Bay: an area where leafy splendour reigns.

The Walk and Points of Interest:

1. Begin at the War Memorial (A) in Queen's Gardens (B).

A. The War Memorial was unveiled on Saturday November 11th, 1922 on the fourth anniversary of the Armistice. The memorial was paid for by public subscription and the lone soldier, sculpted by John Cassidy of Manchester, was described as having, 'No suggestion of the callousness or brutality associated with war.' The lone woman commemorated on the roll of honour, Catherine Williams, was killed whilst serving as a staff nurse.

B. These gardens, originally known as Rydal Field, may seem an oasis on the edge of town but their environmental value has not always been appreciated. In 1933 the council planned to concrete over the site and build a public hall here but were stopped by the strength of local opposition. The council tried again after the war and in 1952 were only prevented by a public enquiry from turning the gardens into a car park. Finally abandoning development plans in 1953 the council honoured the accession of Queen Elizabeth by renaming the park, 'Queen's Gardens'.

2. Follow the diagonal path to the far, right hand corner of the gardens, notice the large buildings (C) facing you, on the other side of Lansdowne Road.

C. This is the heart of Rydal School. The section on the north-western corner, with an octagonal corner turret was originally a detached house called Rydal Mount. Taking its name from the house, the school began here on the 19th September 1885 with 15 pupils. Mr Thomas G. Osborn, a prominent Methodist, was the school's founder and first headmaster. No believer in progressive methods, his own hand written records on pupils

The
·RYDALIAN·

JULY, 1936.

13

are illuminating; some are described as 'bird witted', of one he wrote, 'writing and spelling phenomenal – have never seen worse in a boy of twelve', whilst another was, 'backward and very, very Welsh.' Victorian parents approved and soon pupil numbers rose to around one hundred. Interestingly, the Old Rydalians' magazine recorded in 1905 that only 4 of its 205 members resided in North Wales. When Osborn died in 1910 his son George took over as head, but made rather a mess of things, pupil numbers dropped dramatically and in 1914 George even managed to get himself arrested as a suspected spy. He was reported by a fellow train passenger to be carefully studying maps as they travelled along the coast. The police accepted his explanation that he was not planning a seaborne invasion but marking geography homework. In 1915 George was replaced by the Rev. A.J. Costain, who remained for 34 years. Over the years the school has grown and several 'old boys' have achieved notable success including Brian Kay, the B.B.C. broadcaster, Dafydd Wigley, the Plaid Cymru leader and Duncan Kenworthy, the producer of the film, 'Four Weddings and a Funeral.' Rydal school fees have also grown and successive heads have expressed an anxiety that independent schooling might become the exclusive preserve of the very rich. It is therefore interesting to look back to 1914 when fees were only £88-2-0d. per annum and parental occupations included a pawnbroker, a smack owner, a mungo manufacturer, a buffalo picker manufacturer, a bristle manufacturer and a drysalter.

3. Turn left up Pwllycrochan Avenue and soon notice the White House (D) across the road from the school.

D. The White House is a product of the Arts and Craft movement in architecture. Whilst many Victorian architects were engaged in erecting buildings replete with ornamentation and extravagance to demonstrate the confidence and wealth of the age, others, influenced by William Morris, were keen to study and reproduce the traditional skills and designs of the rural craftsmen. This 'Arts and Crafts' approach is best represented locally by the work of Herbert Luck North of Llanfairfechan, but here is interpreted by the Manchester architect, Alfred Steinthal. The comparatively simple style of the roughcast exterior echoes the plastered exterior of many rural cottages. The flat-roofed garage is a later, unsympathetic addition.

4. Turn right along Oak Drive and then right into Brackley Avenue, notice the second house (E) on your right.

E. Cotswold is an altogether more elaborate example of the Arts and Craft style, again by Steinthal and erected in 1908. The recurrence of Steinthal's designs is a reflection of the success of the Estate in attracting wealthy business people from the north-west of England. His client here was Mrs Benger of the Manchester-based food processing company. Roughcast has again been used but simplicity has been compromised by half-timbering and richly ornamental bargeboards. Such features were widely popular in this period and link the styling of Cotswold to many of the other buildings in this area.

5. Continue to the junction with Lansdowne Road where you turn left and continue across Walshaw Avenue to the corner where Alexandra Road joins on the right. Notice 'The Wren's Nest' (F) on the corner.

F. The Wren's Nest is one of the few later buildings in this West End of Colwyn Bay that has any architectural merit. It was built in 1926 for another client from Manchester, Mrs Guy, whose family owned a motor business; the architect was Colwyn Foulkes. The neo-Georgian style chosen was routinely affected in countless employment exchanges and local government offices across Britain. Here the architect has softened this, often severe, style by the use of several imaginative touches including the use of attractive bricks, an interesting arrangement of windows, a decorative frieze below the eaves and especially the very pretty recessed balcony.

6. Retrace your steps a little and ascend Walshaw Avenue to the top, where it meets Oak Drive. Consider the magnificent edifice (G) opposite.

G. Walshaw lies a long way down the carriageway past its attendant lodge. It was built in 1891 for the Reverend J.G. Haworth in a 'free Jacobethan style' by the architectural partnership of Booth, Chadwick and Porter. This particular Porter was John Merryweather Porter the son of the man who began the development of Colwyn Bay as the land agent of John Pender, the purchaser of the Pwllycrochan Estate. Pender made his money out of laying ocean cables and when one of his cables snapped in mid-Atlantic, in 1875, he had to sell up to survive. A Manchester syndicate, headed by wealthy architect and friend of Sir Henry Irving, Lawrence Booth, bought him out. Soon Booth, J.M. Porter and another Manchester-based architect Thomas Chadwick went into partnership and were designing most of the principal buildings in the rapidly developing town. Walshaw, with its expanses of red brick, half-timbering and decorative terra-cotta is typical of their work. It is now used by Rydal School as a residential building.

7. Continue along Oak Drive, cross the junction with King's Road and then notice the enormous building (H) up on the left.

H. Penrhos Manor, originally Ratonagh, is an equally imposing creation of Booth, Chadwick and Porter. It was built in 1894 for a Manchester businessman, David Gamble J.P. For many years it served as a junior department for Penrhos School but has now been converted into offices and the grounds replanted with 'executive homes.'

8. At the end of Oak Drive turn left up Llanrwst Road. Continuing the steep ascent you soon pass a lodge-house on the right and arrive at a crossroads (I).

I. This was formerly a very important place for travellers. East-west runs the Old Highway leading down to the ancient ferry across the Conwy; north-south runs the old road leading over the hills to the important market town of Llanrwst. On the site, now occupied by two three-storey houses, stood the old Four Crosses Inn. Besides catering to travellers the inn served many other functions for the scattered community. It hosted militia meetings, wakes, tithe auctions, vestry meetings and the collection of rents. Outside there was a pinfold where stray animals were impounded until collected by their owners on payment of a fee. At the beginning of the nineteenth century, under landlady Dolly Evans, the Four Crosses gained something of a reputation. During one particularly boisterous party in 1808, held in an upper room, the revellers stepped so lively that the whole ceiling collapsed, burying the drinkers below. As the coastal route was improved traffic along here gradually declined and the inn finally closed around 1830.

9. Turn right along the Old Highway, stopping when you reach a gatehouse, (J) on the right.

J. This gatehouse and the lodge you noticed previously on Llanrwst Road mark the old entrances to the Flagstaff Estate, which now forms the grounds of the Welsh Mountain Zoo. In the 1890's the 37 acre estate was bought by a wealthy middle aged Manchester surgeon, Walter Whitehead, who intended it to be turned into a paradise for himself and his wife. He engaged Thomas Mawson to create a large mansion house in

17

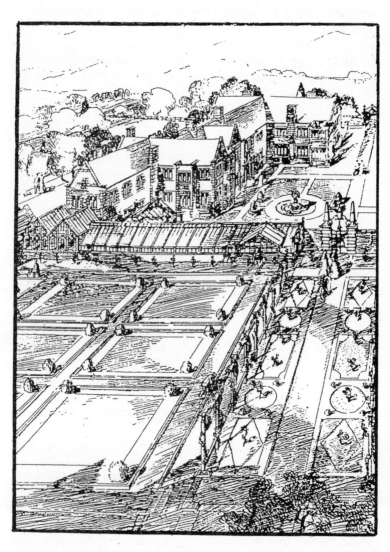

Mawson's original design for the Flagstaff Estate

extensive gardens, of which this gatehouse was the first stage. Unfortunately his wife was so shocked by her visit to this remote outpost of civilisation that she fled back to Manchester and abandoned any thoughts of living with Walter. Whitehead subsequently chose to share his life here with an eccentric German chap who shared Walter's love of all things nautical. They would spend hours together, dressed in sailor caps with telescopes raised to their eyes studying the ships out in Liverpool Bay. To enhance their fantasies they built a 'ship's bridge' in the estate grounds complete with portholes, mast and bunks. When his partner died Walter kept his ashes in his study whilst an identical urn was prepared for his own ashes. Their ashes now lie together in a shared grave, behind the penguin pool. Their 'ship's bridge' has now been incorporated into the 'Lookout Café.' Mawson's grand house was never built and this gatehouse served as home for the medical man and his friend during their years together. When Walter died in 1913 his wife had become sufficiently reconciled to attend his funeral. However, further colour was added to his already eccentric reputation by Mawson's subsequent claims that Whitehead had swindled him out of his original fees and even Walter's obituary emphasised the peculiar claim that he had, 'removed more human tongues than any other surgeon of his time.'

10. Continue along the Old Highway for a further 400 yards until you notice a footpath sign indicating 'Hafodty Lane'. You follow the route indicated to the far left hand corner of the first field where you take the left hand route shown by the signpost. Follow the waymarked path, passing a curious redundant metal step-ladder stile, crossing a similar stile and then passing the rear of the house and metal barns of Hafodty Farm to exit over a stile onto the lane where you turn left and, after 100 yards, turn left again along a footpath at Bryn Hyfryd. After 150 yards you continue ahead down Copthorne Lane rather than take the constricted footpath on the right.

When you reach Llanrwst Road turn left and continue past Seion Methodist Chapel, then take the first right along Pen-y-Bryn Road. Pause after 150 yards and notice a small stone house (K), number 91, on the right.

K. Golf Cottage is a surviving building of the old Colwyn Bay Golf Club. The 1905 'Red Guide' described the club's 100 acre course as, 'the most sporting links in North Wales' but it proved a financial disaster. In the nineteen thirties the Council agreed to step in, buy up the club and operate the links but the war intervened and the plan collapsed. When the club finally closed in 1956 the Council bought the land but sold it to two local businessmen who sought to turn it into a caravan site. A public inquiry turned down this plan but permission was eventually granted for housing development.

11. Continue along Pen-y-Bryn Road but turn left after 200 yards and descend King's Drive for 100 yards before following the sign which indicates a footpath, on the right, through Pwllycrochan Woods (L).

L. Pwllycrochan Woods comprises 40 acres of the old Pwllycrochan Estate that was purchased by the Council on October 1st, 1905 for the enjoyment of the public.

12. Keep to the higher, southern fringe of the woods. After about 800 yards the path descends through a short dog-leg to emerge from the trees at the junction of Pen-y-bryn Road and the Old Highway, where you cross over and descend Woodland Park. Take the first left along Ael-y-bryn Road and after about 80 yards you notice a couple of interesting small detached houses (M) down on the right.

M. Numbers 4 and 6 Ael-y-bryn Road are substantially unaltered, 1930 examples of the work of the celebrated architect

COLWYN BAY GOLF CLUB

18-hole Sporting Links situate on the hill
::   above Pwllycrochan Woods.   ::

The air is exhilarating, and from the highest greens there is said to
be no finer views in Europe.

ENTRANCE FEE:
Ladies and Gentlemen   ..   ..   £1 : 1 : 0

SUBSCRIPTION:
Ladies, £1 : 1 : 0   Gentlemen, £2 : 2 : 0

COUNTY MEMBERS:
Ladies and Gentlemen   ..   ..   £1 : 1 : 0
Lockers, 5/- per year.

GREEN FEES:
Good Friday to September 30th	..	2/6 per day	10/- per week
October 1st to Good Friday	..	2/- ,,	7/6 ,,

Luncheons and Teas Provided
GOLFING REQUISITES STOCKED

A MOTOR runs at convenient times from the Central
Garage, Woodland Road (Fare 6d.)

Steward & Professional: **F. J. FEARNS,** *Hon. Sec.,*
     B. BERRY.   **The Golf House, Colwyn Bay**

Herbert Luck North (1871-1941). He was undoubtedly the most successful architect working in the Arts and Crafts idiom in Wales. Notice the typical roughcast finish, small paned windows, steeply pitched roofs and small hand riven slates. The narrow, vertical staircase window used here is an interesting stylistic feature owing more to the ideas of Scottish architect, Charles Renee Mackintosh, than to North's more typical cottage influences.

13. Continuing past the 'Tradesman's Entrance' of the next house turn right down Coed Pella Road then first left along Queen's Avenue where you notice Beech Holme (N) straight ahead, at the end of the road.

N. Beech Holme is notable for its magnificent Victorian conservatory. The house dates from about 1880, the stables a little later and the whole was acquired by Rydal during the inter-war years.

14. At Beech Holme you turn left and then almost immediately right along Queen's Drive where, set in an extensive private park on the left, is Queen's Lodge (O). A little further along the road, also in large grounds is Outram Lodge (P).

O. Queen's Lodge was built in 1895 for W. Houghton, a Warrington wire magnate. In 1919 it was bought by a manufacturer of india-rubber and cotton who was later enobled as Lord Colwyn. His original name was Fred Smith.

P. Outram Lodge was acquired by Rydal School in 1958. It is another one of Booth, Chadwick and Porter's Tudoresque creations, with half-timbering, manifold gables and decorative stained glass.

.. Pwllycrochan Hotel, ..

15. At the end of Queen's Drive you reach Pwllycrochan Avenue where you are struck by the imposing appearance of the eponymous edifice (Q).

Q. Pwllycrochan was the birthplace of Colwyn Bay. The original mansion house was built in the seventeenth century for Robert Conway but it had become a little neglected when rented by the Reverend James Price in the nineteenth century. Now James was a bit of an eccentric clergyman and his over-enthusiastic DIY 'renovation' work almost rendered the old red brick mansion uninhabitable. His son, curiously known as Old Price, described the scene; 'whole rooms lay exposed to the open-air and had to be guarded by dogs.' When Jane Williams, the owner of the freehold, married Sir David Erskine in 1821 they, perhaps wisely, decided to reclaim their property. The Erskine rebuilding was more drastic but more constructive. The grounds were remodelled with much replanting of the woodland. When the railway arrived, the development value of the Estate lands increased dramatically. On the 12th and 13th September 1865 the great sell-off took place, by auction, at the Erskine Arms, Conwy. John Pender bought the 3,000 acre Estate with its 1¼ miles of 'splendid sea-bathing beach' for £20,000. Pender's agent, John Porter, leased the mansion house and opened it as an hotel in June 1866. Porter bought the freehold when Pender sold out in 1875 and extended the building in 1877 and again in the 1900's. The prestigious hotel prospered until it was requisitioned by the Ministry of Food during World War Two. It was renovated and re-opened in July 1948 but business did not boom and four years later it was sold to Rydal School. It is currently used as a preparatory school.

16. Turning right down Pwllycrochan Avenue, after 60 yards you notice an interesting house (R) on the left.

R. Braeside, with its unusual conically-roofed corner turret, is another building by Booth, Chadwick and Porter. Erected in 1891, the date is inscribed on the exterior amid the decorative terra-cotta frieze. Braeside was home to John Merry Porter (son of the founder of the Pwllycrochan Hotel) until his death in 1942.

17. Take the next right along Combermere Road. Cross over at the end of the road and notice the two houses in front of you, Heathfield (S) on the left and Brendon (T) on the right.

S. Heathfield was designed by John Douglas and his partner D.P. Fordham. Douglas originally came to Colwyn Bay as the chosen architect of John Pender. He practiced in Chester from about 1860 until his death in 1911 and was the region's most accomplished architect. Douglas drew much of his inspiration from the traditional timbering of Cheshire and the Welsh Border and this neo-vernacular approach is evident here. Heathfield was acquired by Rydal School in 1979.

T. Brendon is also by Douglas and Fordham and of about the same 1893 date. The characteristic external timbering is less in evidence but there is some use of broken limestone facing, which is another typical Douglas feature. It has been a Rydal property since 1963.

18. Turn left down Queen's Drive and return to Queen's Gardens.

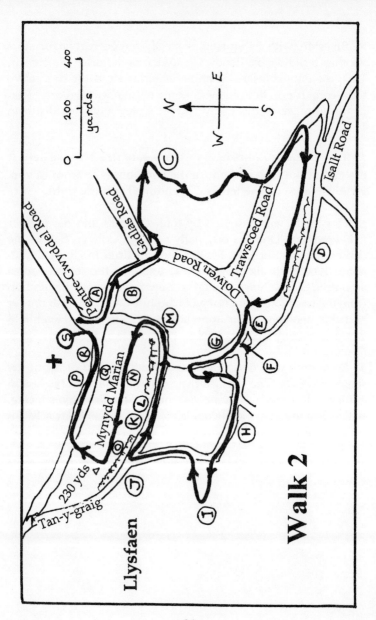

Walk 2

Llysfaen

Llysfaen: a Scattered Celtic Settlement

Walk Number:	Two
Distance:	Four miles
Terrain:	Fairly level, a mixture of paved lanes and muddy field paths
Start:	St Cynfran's Church
Finish:	Circular route
Transport:	Buses 14, 15, 22, 59: approx. four per hour
Refreshments:	Two pubs: the Castle and the Semaphore

Introduction:

English villages are typically made up of cottages clustered around a parish church, a big house, a pub and maybe an old castle. The typical Celtic village is much less centralised, consisting largely of dispersed farms and smallholdings. This is the pattern at Llysfaen. Whilst the ancient settlement pattern has been developed and modified over the years it is still easy to recognise the dispersed nature of the old village. As you walk around you notice small agricultural holdings separated not only by fields but also by stretches of limestone outcropping. The stone may have limited the depth of the soil but over the years it also provided useful building stone. In the nineteenth century this attracted commercial quarrying and led to the erection of several terraces of workers' housing. Even these terraces were small, geographically dispersed and tended to reinforce the scattered settlement pattern. Walking around Llysfaen you soon notice its dispersed character and enjoy a variety of panoramic views across wooded hills and valleys and out across the bay. You ramble from cosy wooded cwms to abandoned quarries, from Mrs Lee's chip-shop to Mrs Hughes' Semaphore Signalling Station.

The Walk and Points of Interest:

1. From the church, walk up the hill, turn left along the road and notice the attractive stone rectory (A) and converted coach-house on the left. Further along, on the right is Ty'n-y-coed (B).

A. This lovely old rectory dates mainly from 1821, when it was erected by the Reverend John Hughes. There had been a previous rectory on the site but it was a much more primitive affair with a thatched roof, 'three rooms and a sellar (sic) below stairs floored with clay and mortar and three rooms and a closet above stairs.' The rectory was extended in 1848 by the Reverend Edward Oldfield whose initials and crest adorn the main entrance. A later incumbent whose sons were both drowned in action during World War One subsequently found the rectory's sea views an unbearable reminder and had to move to a house further inland. The rectory and its coach house have been renovated and sold out of church ownership in recent years.

B. Ty'n-y-coed is a seventeenth century farmhouse with later additions. It originally had a fluted chimney to announce its high status to all. In an earlier age to possess a chimney at all was a sure sign of having made it, but by 1600 chimneys were ten a penny (not quite) and ornamentation was required to impress.

2. Just past Gadlas Road, you follow a footpath which passes alongside a semi-detached house. Follow the left-hand fork for 200 yards where you cross a stile on the right and walk along the field edge alongside Plas-yn-Llysfaen (C) and its farm.

C. It is difficult to get a good view of Plas-yn-Llysfaen. It has a typical Georgian façade although the cellars retain features of its earlier origins. It is sometimes referred to as Plas yr Esgob and may have originally formed part of an estate granted to the Bishop of Bangor by Edward 1st, for baptising the infant Prince of Wales. This would push its origins back to the thirteenth century.

3. After 100 yards you cross a stile, with a disused quarry to your right, keeping alongside the left-hand boundary; after 25 yards you pass through a kissing-gate and continue along the path for 200 yards before you cross a metal stile, take a sharp right-turn, then a left where the path opens out and there is a smallholding on either side. Trawscoed (very minor) Road is 60 yards ahead and when you reach it you turn right and notice a panoramic view south over the hills. Continue for 200 yards, passing Bryn Defaid on the right, before turning right over a stile which is signed as part of the North Wales Path. For the next 600 yards the way is signed so just keep to roughly the same contour level with the field boundary to your right. After about 300 yards you notice, far below on the left, a road heading south, then the next farm you see on the left is Isallt (D).

D. Despite its plethora of ugly tin sheds Isallt is an important early seventeenth century farmstead. There is the usual clutch of evidential architectural features, such as stop-chamfered beams but also a fascinating copy of the original deeds have been preserved, written in Latin and in scroll form.

4. Soon you cross a stile, alongside a single storey cottage, Craig Lwyd, turn right, pass a few houses and then go left along the road until you notice a chapel (E).

E. Tabor Baptist Chapel, opened in November 1884, stands as a tribute to the old Baptist community of nineteenth century Llysfaen. The stone was carried to the site by local farmers and worked by committed quarrymen. The architectural plans were commissioned by that fiery old radical Spinther James. The chapel prospered and was enlarged in 1911, when a schoolroom was added.

5. Don't walk down past the chapel but turn right along Tan-y-Graig Road, noticing Jenning's Plant Services (G) on the right and a long building (F), a little nearer, on the left.

F. The front section of this building, facing the road as it branches left, was Junction Stores. The rear part, with the loft-door, was used as a storehouse whilst the single storey section, with the two modern windows has served a variety of owners and functions: Mr Evans' cobblers, Mr Williams' saddlery and Mrs Lee's chip-shop.

G. The Jennings Plant Services building used to be the Bod Hyfryd Inn. The last landlord was a Mr Hughes who served his last pint here in the nineteen-twenties, when Mr and Mrs Jones were running Junction Stores.

6. Follow the sign ahead on the left towards Hwylfa Dafydd Farm but keep on the track, bearing left past the front of Hwylfa Terrace. Turn right when you reach Bwlch y Gwynt Road. Walk along the upper terrace but notice the large building (H) below, just to the right of the junction with Dolwen Road.

H. This was Bryniau Cochion Farm whose name means Red, or bloody, Hills. This is taken as a reference to savage battles that have taken place in these uplands. In 818, for example, there was an attack on the Saxon King Egbert who led an army this way to attack Ynys Môn. In 1245 Dafydd ap Llewelyn ab Iorwerth is said to have repulsed Henry III's army here, when the English army was on its way to attack Deganwy.

7. Continue along Bwlch y Gwynt Road until Geulan Road forks off to the right, here you follow the lane straight ahead. Soon you reach Pebi farmhouse (I), where you turn right down a footpath indicated by a gap in the undergrowth, a few yards before reaching the farm gate.

I. Pebi is referred to in old documents and maps as Pebig but the origins of its name remain obscure. The left-hand higher section was the original seventeenth century farmhouse but little of the original detailing has been preserved although the inglenook fireplace is believed to exist behind later brickwork and plaster.

8. Descending through the overgrown vegetation you soon reach a lovely little stone cottage where you turn right and continue along the lane in front of the cottage for 130 yards, turning left along Geulan Road and continuing for 200 yards where you join Tan-y-graig Road, with Tŷ-ucha Farm (J) on the left.

J. Tŷ-ucha is another seventeenth century farmhouse and has retained more of its original character than Pebi. Before the war its fields were often filled with the bell tents of Boy Scouts and Boys' Brigade groups, who regularly held their summer camp here. Tŷ-ucha has also retained its old slate-topped roadside churn-stand from the days before milk was collected by industrial-sized milk-tankers.

9. Turn right and walk along Tan-y-graig Road, noticing on the left the Castle Inn (K) and, a little further on, a short terrace of houses, Storehouse (L).

K. The Castle Inn has been a pub for 300 years although the original building has been much extended in the twentieth century.

L. Storehouse Terrace used to accommodate a little parade of shops which included Mrs Parry's Dressmakers, Mrs Davies' General Stores and a cobblers run by Mr Hams. Tragedy is no stranger here. One day in October 1860 John Roberts was at home here when he received a visit from his brother, Owen. It was the last time he was to see him alive, for Owen was soon to be shot dead by a local gamekeeper (see Walk 3). On 15th May 1919 William Jones was not at home when fate struck at number 3, Storehouse. William had been having a difficult time since his demobilisation from the army the previous year. Six months after his return his wife had died, leaving him to bring up six little children. He had already been sent papers by the police warning him about drinking and leaving his children unsupervised. Unfortunately, William could neither read nor write in English or Welsh. His uncle, Robert Jones, who had been discharged from the army after losing an arm, lived next door at number 4. He heard screaming, and running in, was horrified to see four year old Rhoda Jones on fire. He attempted to smother the flames but it was too late. Little Rhoda had fallen into the open fire and was burnt alive.

10. Continue past Manchester House (M), on the right.

M. The name, 'Manchester House' reflects the former predominance of that city in the cloth trades, for this used to be a flourishing draper's shop run by Mr Evans and his sister. Goods on sale ranged from drapery and clothes to knitting wool and footwear.

11. Follow the road round before turning left to follow the rough track that ascends Mynydd Marian to the Signal Station (N).

N. Llysfaen's Signal Station is a rare survivor. It has retained much of its character and setting. Originally erected in 1827 and

rebuilt in 1841, it formed a link in a chain of signal stations stretching from Holyhead to Liverpool. Although most signal chains constructed around the world were developed for military purposes, this was an enterprise planned and financed privately by the Liverpool Port Authority. Liverpool decided to invest in such cutting-edge communications to compete with other ports whose approaches were less adversely affected by difficult winds and shallow sand banks. Liverpool had good inland connections to the manufacturing centres of the North of England and Wales, and it aimed to use signalling technology to enhance its appeal. Merchants could exploit this network to track the progress of their cargoes long before they reached port. This gave them an opportunity to plan unloading, onward transport of goods, and reloading of cargoes for export with maximum efficiency. The message was conveyed along the signal chain using a system of flags or semaphore. By the second half of the nineteenth century the development of the electric telegraph made this visual system of communication redundant but, fortunately, this station survived as a domestic dwelling.

12. Continue following the rough path along the top of the Marian with marvelous views out over the bay. After 300 yards you notice a covered reservoir (O) alongside a triangulation point which marks the 230 yards elevation point.

O. This reservoir was constructed in 1911 to provide a reliable piped water supply for villagers who had previously depended on a variety of springs and wells. The rock was quarried out, lined with concrete and covered with a brick-arch roof, providing a capacity of 132,000 gallons (600,000 litres).

13. Continue along a rough path towards the houses down on the right where you then walk along a lane which soon meets Ffordd-y-Llan where you turn right. After 300 yards you notice the Semaphore Inn (P) on the left, with the old village school (Q) almost opposite.

P. The Semaphore Inn began life as Lodge Farm but gradually began to expand its commercial activities. In the 1920's Mr Parry had a butcher's shop here. He also ran a milk round and had a public house licence. There used to be a public road leading down past the Lodge to connect with Abergele Road but in Mr Parry's time the council swapped this right of way for the development of Highlands Road in an arrangement made with Raynes' quarry.

Q. The National School, built in 1871, was financed by local bigwigs to promote the religious principles of the Established Anglican Church. Although school attendance was compulsory, it was not free until 1891 and parents had to provide a couple of pence a week to pay the fees. All teaching was in English although Welsh was the everyday language of the village, and it is hardly surprising that few children or their parents were very enthusiastic about school learning. At planting and haymaking pupils were more likely to be found in the fields than the classroom. The authorities did not approve of this but were themselves keen enough to cancel lessons in order to celebrate significant events of the social calendar. A tea party and fete were held to celebrate the coming of age of Mr E. Wynne, Cefn and another to celebrate the wedding of Miss Hesketh and Lord Cochrane. For Queen Victoria's Golden Jubilee in 1887, ' the school children mustered in the playground . . . where each received a medal. They then marched round the base of the hill carrying flags and singing the National Anthem and a jubilee song. They made a short stay at the rectory and after singing again they marched to church where a service was held. In the afternoon a substantial tea was given to them all.' To mark Victoria's Diamond Jubilee lessons were cancelled for the whole week.

14. From the old school continue along Ffordd-y-Llan past a small garage-like building (R) at the corner of the churchyard to the church (S).

R. The building in the south-east corner of the churchyard was erected in 1880 to accommodate a horse-drawn hearse. The arched, gothic doorway is typical of buildings designed to serve the Anglican Church. Llysfaen's Victorian hearse was kept here until the 1960's when it was sold to a private buyer and its whereabouts are now unknown.

S. St Cynfran's Church was built in 1377 on the foundations of an earlier church but by Queen Victoria's time it was recorded that, 'rain was coming in and the birds of the air were able to fly in and out through the roof.' In 1870 a drastic programme of renovation was carried out; the walls were rebuilt, the bell-turret, porch, windows, pews and flooring were all replaced. Although a new slate roof was also installed the original fourteenth century roof timbers remain along with their oak pegs. There are three features of the churchyard that are especially worth seeking out. The war memorial, near the gate, has an especially fitting memorial inscription. The verse, or englyn, was composed by Hedd Wyn, (Ellis Evans), who won the Bardic Chair at the 1917 National Eisteddfod. At the ceremony the chair was draped in black as Hedd Wynn had already fallen as a victim of the Great War. About six graves from the gate, lies Mary Hughes, keeper of the Telegraph Station in mid-Victorian times. Beyond the church, just one grave away from the path that leads to the first cemetery extension, lies Elijah Wood, one of the gypsies whose brightly painted, bow-topped wooden caravans were once a familiar part of Llysfaen life. Elijah died in the rectory coach-house in 1899 as a guest of the Rev. Robert Jones.

Exploring Glan Conwy's Fascinating History

Walk Number:	Three
Distance:	Five miles
Terrain:	Field paths and paved lanes, some moderate ascents
Start:	Glan Conwy railway station
Finish:	Circular route
Transport:	Six return train services each day between Colwyn Bay and Glan Conwy, change at Llandudno Junction
Refreshments:	There are two pubs and a Chinese chip shop near Glan-Conwy railway station, and a café at Felin Isaf

Introduction:

Around the year 500 Saint Bride sailed from Ireland on a piece of turf. She was eventually cast ashore on a rocky promontory in the Conwy estuary where she later constructed a simple Celtic chapel. Her landing place became known as Trwyn Capel and the settlement that grew up around it became Llansanffraid Glan Conwy, or the church, or enclosure, of Saint Bride alongside the Conwy. The story may be apocryphal but the foundation of the village in the early sixth century is substantiated by other accounts. Throughout most of its long history Llansanffraid has looked to the river as its main highway. Evidence of this maritime past remains along with a Neolithic tomb, three water-mills, a model farm and a tale of legal murder.

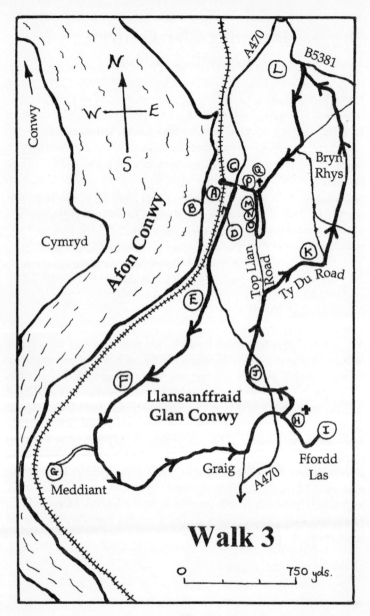

Walk 3

The Walk and Points of Interest:

A. The railway station opened on the 17th June 1863 and was initially called Llansainffraid but renamed Glan Conway in 1865. An interesting twentieth century feature of the station was the camping coach, which was deployed here in the summer months. Holidaymakers rented it to use as a caravan enjoying the wonderful river and mountain views and the convenience of nearby rail travel. The station was actually closed down in December 1964 but reopened in 1970 because of the increased population of the area. The frequency of passenger trains is now similar to that of the 1860's but ironically the best service ever operated in the years just before closure, with up to 14 return services a day in 1960!

1. From the station platform look left, towards Afon Conwy and notice a rocky promontory (B) protruding from the mud, about 30 yards away.

B. These rocks mark Saint Bride's, or Bridget's, legendary landing place. Besides building a church here St Bride also chose this spot to perform a service of more immediate value to locals. The people had suffered crop failure and were starving when St Bride responded to their pleas for help with a curious request for them to cut rushes. When she cast their bundles into the river they miraculously transformed into shoals of fish which the villagers ravenously devoured. Sceptics consider this story as likely as that of her original voyage from Ireland on a piece of turf, but there is no doubt that this was indeed the site of the original church. By 1729 the old church of St Bridget was in ruins and was subsequently rebuilt higher up in the village.

2. Leaving the station, walk up towards the village but notice the old stone building on your left (C), before the main road.

C. This is the last surviving warehouse from the days of sail. Dating from the eighteenth century it was used as a temporary storehouse for sea-going imports and exports through the port of Llansanffraid Glan Conwy. Before the railway arrived, Glan Conwy was an important local shipping centre. Cargo boats plied between here and Ireland, Chester and Liverpool as well as ports further along the valley. Boats were built here until the end of the eighteenth century and along the river here were boatyards, sailmakers, chandlers, carriers and all the other associated trades.

3. Turn right along the main road, first noticing the Conwy Vale pub (D) on the right, and then after a further 500 yards turn right down Garth Road (E).

D. The Conwy Vale was the Wheatsheaf until the end of the nineteenth century. On the 8th October 1860 it was also the scene of a coroner's inquest into the deliberate and shocking killing of Owen Roberts in the grounds of Bryn Eisteddfod, which you will visit presently and where all will be revealed.

E. Garth Road is thought to follow the course of a Roman road, which led to a point above Tal-y-cafn, where the Romans crossed to their camp at Canovium (Caerhun). The significance of this route was partly confirmed by a find of Roman coins in Glan Conwy in 1940.

4. After 300 yards turn right along a lane which passes between Garth and Llys-y-gwynt. Soon you reach Pantygangen farm where you go through the farm-gate, turn right through the farmyard and then left along the footpath. After 200 yards you reach a kissing gate at the edge of a field. Cross the field by following the higher, left-hand boundary. At the far end descend a little, past a kissing gate to a massive rock (F).

F. This massive rock is the capstone of Hendre Waelod Burial Chamber, which has slipped from its vertical supporting stones. Referred to locally as Allor Moloch, (or Moloch's Altar), it was erected about 2,500 B.C. Originally it would have contained a burial and been covered with a mound of earth and stones.

5. Return to the kissing gate above the cromlech, pass through and continue along the lower boundary of the next field to a kissing gate at the far end. Now follow the track, which bears left into another field. Keep alongside the left-hand hedge to exit onto a metalled lane over a wooden stile. Pause here and notice a lane to your right which leads to Meddiant Farm (G), (don't descend this private lane).

G. Two hundred years ago Meddiant was not just a farmhouse but also a school. The proprietor was Hugh Williams whose most successful pupil was his own grandson, Hugh Hughes. Hughes is famed for his collection of sixty topographical engravings published under the title, 'The Beauties of Cambria' and inscribed, 'Meddiant, 1823.' He was also a talented portraitist but by 1832 had become an out-and-out radical and devoted himself to a range of progressive causes. He supported Catholic Emancipation and was expelled from the Methodist Church for his pains. He opposed all forms of Church Establishment and was vehemently against tithe payments. As a radical speaker he was a great asset, but as a satirical cartoonist he was invaluable. He lampooned the commission appointed in 1847 to, 'inquire into the state of education in the Principality of Wales' to great effect. Their report, in its official blue binding, was exposed as a cynical, supercilious condemnation of Welsh schools, Welsh children and in fact, all things Welsh. Its production became known in Wales as, Brad y Llyfrau Gleision – (The Treason of the Blue Books).

6. Turn left, away from Meddiant, and continue along the lane for 300 yards until you reach a T-junction with a modern bungalow ahead. Turn left and follow the road around until you reach the hamlet of Graig. Keep left and follow the road down to the junction with the A470. Cross over and ascend the minor road opposite. Soon you notice a chapel (H). Go through the gate to the graveyard at the rear.

H. Salem Baptist Chapel, founded in 1786, played an important role in establishing the cause in the area. Two interesting aspects of this history are noted on the white, draped-urn memorial, near the corner of the chapel. Margaret Owen is remembered for keeping alive the cause in Llandudno. For many years she was the only Baptist in town, yet she faithfully walked all the way from her home on the Great Orme to chapel here every Sunday. Anne Evans made an even greater sacrifice for her faith: she refused to obey her husband's demands that she abandon her Baptist beliefs, so he beat her to death. Notice also the nearby gravestone of the Roberts family of Factory House: you will visit this next, but first return to the front of the chapel. Look for a memorial over the chapel-house entrance identifying this as the birthplace of the sculptor John Gibson (1790-1866). This oft-repeated claim is in fact an error, for Gibson was actually born in Conwy. He moved here with his parents when he was two years old.

7. Facing the chapel, turn right and walk for 150 yards until you see a complex of old buildings on the right. Go through the metal farm gate opposite and cross the field alongside the right hand hedge until you reach another gate, where you pause and look at the white house and stone barn (I) across the stream.

I. This was Felin Lifio, the saw mill, otherwise called Factory House. Powered by the waters of Nant Garreg-ddu, you might just make-out the old waterwheel, covered in creepers, at the front of the old barn-like mill. In the nineteenth century these waters were dammed and channelled and provided motive power not just for the saw-mill here, but also for two corn mills further downstream. The public footpath officially crosses a footbridge here and passes alongside the mill to reach a country lane leading to Felin Ucha. Selfishness and neglect now denies people proper access to this delightful route. I have included this dead-end partly to provide a comprehensive look at all three mills but also to exemplify part of the historical process by which we are denied access to our shared heritage. The footbridge was swept away by floods and now neither the council, nor the landowner, seem prepared to replace it.

8. Retrace your steps to a point just past the chapel where an old blacksmith-made gate marks the entrance to another route to Felin Ucha. Walk through the gate and along the footpath

Felin Isaf provides an historic and picturesque refreshment place

and soon you meet an amazing scene, huge mobile cranes everywhere. Continue over the bridge and negotiate your way left. Soon you arrive in a comparatively open space with the old three-storey mill building (Felin Uchaf) on your right. Continuing ahead, exit down a quiet road, passing a couple of old single storey cottages; you turn left past Nev's Garage (the old smithy) and cross the A470. Continue along the lane opposite and after 200 yards you follow a footpath on the right. You cross a delightful stream and emerge on the edge of the lawn of Felin Isaf (J).

J. Felin Isaf is a welcome contrast to the two mills upstream. Whilst Felin Lifio is in romantic decline and Felin Uchaf is deluged by industrial debris, Felin Isaf is beautifully restored and maintained and welcomes visitors. Although the public footpath allows a glimpse of the complex it really is worth buying a ticket and having a comprehensive look, it also makes an ideal refreshment stop. Felin Isaf actually comprises two adjacent mills, a two-storey clover mill of 1680 and a grain mill of 1740, which was in commercial production until 1942. Both of these mills retain their original machinery, although much restored. Another part of the site is occupied by a nineteenth century oat kiln, a very rare survivor. This was used for driving off the moisture in the crop before the grinding process.

9. Walk around the lawn to a wooden footbridge which you cross and then ascend a short driveway to once again reach the A470. Cross over and ascend the minor road which is almost opposite. After 300 yards turn right onto an even more minor road and continue for another 300 yards until you notice a large farm alongside the road on the left, Tŷ-du (K).

K. Tŷ-du was built in 1857 as a model farm for Whitehall Dod (1823-1878), who also owned a lot of land at Llandrillo-yn-Rhos. Model farms were built as a kind of rural factory where the farm buildings and functions were carefully integrated to promote maximum efficiency. The original courtyard layout of the outbuildings has been retained. The chimney marks the position of the brewhouse, which has kept most of its original fittings. Also ranged around the courtyard are the stables, the steam engine house and the pulley wheels, which protrude from the external walls.

10. Follow the road for 100 yards as it bears left and then cross a wooden stile, on the right. Soon ascend the steep bank, on the left and at the top continue to the ridge, on a diagonal course. You should see a large farmhouse in the distance, which indicates your general direction across the field. Exit by the kissing gate onto a lane, turn right and after 15 yards cross over and follow the sign along the farm lane to Tyn-y-coed. Go through the gate on the right of the house and follow the upper green-lane for 600 yards. Now cross the wooden footbridge, which was installed by Conwy Council to facilitate this walk, a welcome contrast to the situation at Melin Lifio. Climb the ladder stile and continue alongside the right-hand fence past Ffordd farmhouse, across the lane and then along the rear of some barns. You are heading for a wide gap in the hedge near a lone tree, then cross the large field ahead aiming for the far right end of the woodland. After 200 yards you exit through a kissing gate onto a metalled road, just above the main entrance of Bryn Eisteddfod (L).

L. Bryn Eisteddfod is the major house of the area. The name comes from a putative Druidic stone in the grounds. The property is so architecturally and historically significant that its constituent parts merit 10 separate statutory listings: including the largely Regency main house, the walled pleasure garden of 1760, the early nineteenth century cartshed and stables, two 1833 lodges, the elegant access bridge of 1841, the walled kitchen garden and the nineteenth and early twentieth century glasshouses. The house is now home to local historian Michael Senior, but the estate lands have been retained by the family who occupied Bryn Eisteddfod in 1860, when it was the scene of a deadly shooting. At four o'clock on the morning of Sunday 7th October 1860 the Bryn Eisteddfod gamekeeper, Edward Petch, and the under-keeper, William Jones, spotted poachers netting a rabbit on Estate land. The keepers were both armed with loaded shotguns. The poachers were unarmed. Petch claimed he shouted out, 'Hello lads' and was promptly attacked and disarmed by two poachers. Jones claimed that he was beaten and chased by three men who repeatedly hit him with sticks causing much pain and bruising. Yet when the dust had settled one of the poachers, Owen Roberts, of Llysfaen, lay dead from a gunshot wound from Petch's weapon, his, 'liver was torn to pieces . . . the right kidney was lacerated . . . the diaphragm and right lung were pierced through and . . . a rib was broken.' When Jones, the under-keeper, was ordered to strip and have his wounds examined, 'behold there were no marks at all.' Despite their unconvincing testimony, the keepers were not tried for killing the unarmed poacher, who was supposed to have taken Petch's gun and shot himself! It was not explained why Jones, who also had a loaded shotgun stood by and let this happen. The official verdict was, 'Found shot . . . but no evidence to prove whether wilfully or accidentally, or by whom.' It seems the keepers got away with murder. To the estate-owners and legal authorities, pheasants were more valuable than peasants. With the victim's widow, Emma, now left to bring up two children unaided, the Coroner eloquently reflected the sympathies of the authorities in his summing up; 'Poachers without exception are as a class the most disreputable on the face of the earth. They are scum...they will commit any sin – any crime. Too lazy to work . . . the idea of thieving is grounded in them . . . They poach for no other reason but that they may have wherewith to gratify their passion for drink.'

11. Return to the field alongside Bryn Eisteddfod but this time follow the path signed to the right, passing alongside the edge of the woodland for the length of the first field. Go through the kissing gate and then bear left alongside the hedge-boundary to another kissing gate. Continue until you exit through yet another kissing gate onto a metalled lane. Turn right and continue descending, right at the T-junction and then continue until turning left opposite the church, along Top Llan Road. Notice the following, all on the right: about 20 yards along look up at a plaque depicting a sailing ship on the wall of house number eight (M), a little further on notice number twenty-four (N), and the further still, Plas Tirion (O).

M. When Llansanffraid was a vibrant river-port this was the home of Captain Robert Jones, who was lost whilst sailing on the Margaret Elizabeth, possibly off Penmon Point.

N. Number 24, Top Llan was the previously the White Horse, one of fifteen village pubs that no longer serve beer. Before the railway and the lower road were built this was the main road to Llanrwst and this old inn catered for travellers as well as locals. It is thought to have been constructed as an hostelry in 1630 but given a modern frontage in the nineteenth century. Internally it retains the original beams.

O. Plas Tirion is an elegant late Georgian house of 1812. It provides an interesting link with Llansanffraid's maritime past, having been built for a local sea captain. Many period features have been retained with original slate flagged floors to the hall and former kitchens.

12. Retrace your steps to the church (P) and churchyard (Q) before descending Church Street to return to the station.

P. This was the site chosen for St Ffraid's Church after the original crumbled into Afon Conwy. The building is largely the work of architect John Welch and was erected in 1839-40. The style is a kind of failed Romanesque reminiscent of the church at Betws-yn-Rhos, which Welch also designed. Some fine medieval glass from the previous church has been incorporated in the West window.

Q. There are several interesting memorials in the churchyard. Just opposite the church door is a memorial to John Tarrey who died aged 2 years in 1831, a victim of the sinking of the pleasure steamer Rothsay Castle near Llandudno. The vessel should never have put to sea, the captain was drunk, the timbers rotten, the pumps useless and the only bucket fell overboard when the crew tried to bail out the incoming waters. The infant's mother, Alice, is buried at St Tudno's, on the Great Orme, whilst little John's lifeless body was cast ashore at Glan Conwy. Notice a tall obelisk to the rear of the church, marking the grave of John Evans who was born in the village in 1814. He was a prolific writer and translator and a popular adjudicator at Eisteddfodau. Behind the church, notice the massive vaults of the squirearchy of Bryn Eisteddfod, who are actually all buried inside the church, under the vestry. Some suggest a monument that is outwardly impressive but without content is a fitting memorial to the local gentry.

Playhouses, Picture Palaces and Pleasure Gardens

Walk Number:	Four
Distance:	Two and a half miles
Terrain:	Seaside promenade, town trails and parkland
Start:	Colwyn Bay Public Hall, Abergele Road
Finish:	Circular route
Transport:	Centrally located
Refreshments:	The Picture House, Prince's Drive, Colwyn Bay

Introduction:

The Official 1938 Guide to Colwyn Bay promised, 'An extensive variety of amusements and recreations . . . there is always something going on . . . comfortably appointed cinemas where the world's finest pictures are exhibited . . . a Repertory Theatre where all the latest London plays are presented . . . in the Pier Pavilion an excellent Concert Party performs twice daily . . . there is an an Alfresco Stand on the promenade where Variety Entertainments are given, the municipal orchestra performs every morning and afternoon on the pier and the Colwyn Borough Band gives frequent open-air concerts in Eirias Park.' Things are quieter now, there's no Alfresco Entertainment on the promenade, the municipal orchestra has disbanded and the world no longer exhibits its finest pictures in Colwyn Bay. Yet much remains to interest and amuse the curious pedestrian.

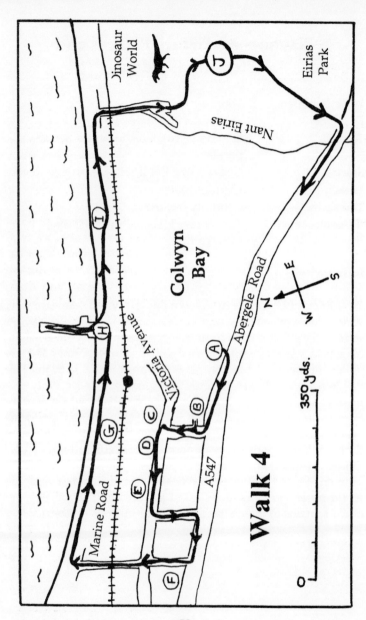

Walk 4

Colwyn Bay

Dinosaur World

Eirias Park

Nant Eirias

Abergele Road

Victoria Avenue

Marine Road

A547

350 yds.

0

The Walk and Points of Interest:

1. Begin at the Public Hall (A) in Abergele Road.

A. The Public Hall opened around 1880 and was originally used as a venue for a wide variety of meetings and events, political, social and religious. Until the opening of the pier in 1900 the Public Hall was the only permanent venue for entertainment in Colwyn Bay although various entrepreneurs put on temporary, open-air performances in summer, especially along the sea front. In early 1897 the Public Hall provided the first opportunity for local audiences to see the marvel of moving pictures. The film show was organised by that great pioneer of the medium, Arthur Cheetham, who returned the following year on Monday and Tuesday, June 20th and 21st 1898 to exhibit moving pictures of Colwyn Bay. These had been filmed by Cheetham himself. These shows were a great success but Rhyl-based Cheetham continued touring and eventually set up his first permanent cinema in his home town. He returned in September 1908 with his 'Silvograph' and this began a period of many years in which the Public Hall operated as a permanent cinema. Harry Reynolds took over the lease in 1909 and completely refurbished the building, which was, 'repainted, decorated, new plush tip-up seats fitted and electric lighting installed.' Following the old practice of the theatres the front seats were still the most expensive at a shilling with seats at the rear for only three pence. In 1930 there was a serious fire and the building had to be extensively repaired before reopening as the 'New Rialto.' In 1936 a Mr Stanley Ravenscroft brought a company of repertory actors to the theatre for a nine week season but the run was so successful that the company decided to stay. Packed audiences continued until well after the war but by 1950 empty seats became all too common. In 1951 the theatre closed for the winter season and for the next few years it remained difficult to continue regular repertory work. When

The end of a Perfect Day

West End Plays to entertain you ... to intrigue or mystify you ... to make you laugh or cry ... and presented by a first rate cast under the direction of Geoffrey Hastings ... mid-week programme changes ... bar and cafe ... in ones or twos, family groups, or special parties ... a perfect end to any day is a visit to The Prince of Wales ...

THE *Prince of Wales* THEATRE

ABERGELE ROAD, COLWYN BAY. *Manager:* P. Yates. *Tel.* 2668

Stanley Ravenscroft decided to retire in 1958 it looked as if the theatre might close down altogether. Fortunately, the Borough Council stepped in and bought the building in January 1959. The theatre was renovated, reopened on 11th June 1959 and renamed 'The Prince of Wales Theatre'. The new theatre manager was Geoffrey Hastings who continued the repertory tradition. Nowadays the theatre offers a wide variety of entertainment.

2. Continue along Abergele Road for about 200 yards, pass the top of Station Road and pause outside the hardware shop (B).

B. This shop opened as the Colwyn Bay Cinema at 3pm on Friday 22nd December 1911. The site had previously been occupied by the coaching business of J.F. Francis, which incorporated a redundant Methodist chapel. This was the first permanent moving picture theatre in Colwyn Bay and the proprietor was our old friend from the Public Hall film show, Arthur Cheetham. Cheetham was a typical early showman, full of self-promotion, exaggeration and downright lies but he was also the greatest pioneer of film and cinema in Wales. With a typical flourish, Cheetham donated the whole of his first day's takings to worthy local causes, having made great play of this in his initial advertising. The architect for the scheme was Colwyn Foulkes who managed to incorporate part of the old chapel into the new cinema. 'The ceiling of the entrance is domed over and exquisitely modelled in plaster and the pavement is of Roman Glass Mosaic of rich and beautiful colours. A feature of the entrance is the illuminated sign of unique design, which takes the form of the prow of a Viking ship, projecting from the façade . . . inside the hall, one is first attracted by the massive old oak beams supporting the roof. A frieze, of beautifully modelled plaster, surrounds the walls and continues along the balcony front, out of which every here and there, juts a quaint little lantern of Cathedral glass. The seating is entirely of the tip-up variety in all parts of the hall and these will be found perfectly comfortable . . . it can be truthfully said that the Colwyn Bay Cinema is the Last Word in picture theatres.' In later years the cinema was called the 'Cosy' and this name seemed appropriate to patrons attracted by its small, intimate size and its double, even more intimate 'courting' seats at the back. First to open and first to close, as audiences declined in the 1950's, the Cosy closed its doors to filmgoers for the last time on Saturday 28th May 1955.

3. Before leaving this point do notice the attractive Edwardian shop front of the tobacconists on the right of the old cinema. Walk a few yards in the opposite direction, turn right down Penrhyn Road and first right along the rear service lane, continue to where the lane turns left and then pause below the security camera. From here you can detect the stonework of the original chapel and the brick-built film projection box high up on the rear wall. This was essential to meet new cinema regulations introduced in 1909 to limit the effects of fires caused by the highly flammable early film stock. Retrace your steps to Penrhyn Road and walk down to the lower end; cross over Prince's Drive and pause in front of 'K F C'. In Victorian times there were no buildings here, just fields which occasionally provided a venue for al-fresco film shows (C).

C. In 1900 the 'Wargraph' gave the people of Colwyn Bay their first opportunity to see moving pictures of Britain's war against the Boers. The scenes were projected outdoors on summer evenings in the field opposite the Metropole Hotel, alongside the Railway Station. The public were mightily moved by stirring scenes of drama from the South African War, even though much of the 'Actual Battle Scenes' were re-enacted in the calm between the fighting and sometimes even in the fields and gardens of Britain.

THE

Princess Theatre

Colwyn Bay

TELEPHONE 32557   Proprietor GEORGE H. KENYON

DECEMBER
1928

Monthly Programme

4. Continuing along Prince's Drive, walking away from the station, you quickly notice an old cinema reborn as a pub (D).

D. The Princess Theatre opened on Wednesday 1st July 1914 and attempted to attract potential customers from the existing cinema by offering a superior standard of comfort. 'The entrance hall, with its artistic Italian Terazzo flooring, has its walls and ceiling panelled with beautiful ornamental moulding. Comfort has been considered in every detail, and the seating consists of luxurious spring seats upholstered in rich blue velvet and suitably numbered for advance booking. Fixed on the roof of the building are four large ventilators of the Boyle's patent air pump type, which draw all the foul air, smoke etc. through six ornamental grilles in the ceiling, leaving the atmosphere cool and free from all impurities.' In 1932 the cinema was remodelled in the fashionable neo-Egyptian art-deco style. In 1981 it was again remodelled, but this time in the deeply unfashionable, 'eyes-down, look-in' bingo style. In 1999 much of that 1932 cinema styling was restored. Films are no longer shown but the building is once again a pleasure to behold and is recommended as an appropriate refreshment stop.

5. Continue walking along Prince's Drive until you reach the Post Office building (E).

E. The Arcadia Theatre previously stood on the left of the Post Office building. It opened at 8pm on Saturday 7th June 1919 and in recognition of the proximity of the war's end it was initially referred to as, The Victory Theatre. It was erected for Catlins who had previously organised entertainments, in season, on the promenade. The architect was Sidney Colwyn Foulkes. The façade was rather classical in appearance but with a sort of Parisian influence. There were 1,100 tip-up seats upholstered in crimson plush, electric lights and 'scientific ventilation'. The theatre also incorporated a café promising 'popular prices'. The

ARCADIA

COLWYN BAY.

Managing Director ... ... W. CATLIN.
Manager and Director of Entertainments ... ... FRANK A. TERRY.
Resident Manager ... ... Tel. 265 ... ... WALLACE KENNEDY.

Catlin's Royal Pierrots.

PROGRAMME - - 2d.

CONTROLLING   The Arcadia Theatre and Cafe, **COLWYN BAY.**
The Arcadia Theatre and Cafe, Llandudno.

Also at **SCARBOROUGH :**
The Arcadia, The Palladium Picture House,
The Arcadia Restaurant and Buffet, and
The Kings-Cliffe Holiday Camp for Men.

opening show featured the 'Royal Pierrots' directed by Sidney Frere who eventually left to run the old Playhouse cinema, in Rhos-on-Sea. After the Second World War the Arcadia regularly offered a venue for the shows of the amateur operatic societies of the town. Renamed the Wedgewood in the 1970's, closure and demolition finally arrived in February 1981.

6. Turn left up Mostyn Road and continue to the junction with Conwy Road. The flats on the right occupy the site of Colwyn Bay's grandest cinema (F).

F. The Odeon opened on the site now occupied by Swn-y-Môr flats at 8pm on Saturday, April 25th, 1936. The opening film was, The Ghost Goes West, starring Robert Donat and Jean Parker. There were special prices for this initial performance with the Grand Circle costing a heady two shillings and sixpence. The Odeon not only followed the national chain's lead of creating architecturally cutting-edge cinemas, it excelled the brief. The Colwyn Bay Odeon was one of the best cinema buildings ever built in Britain, unlike its nondescript replacement. The style was confidently modern with biscuit coloured external tiling, set off with black coping, coloured banding and thin grey-green bricks. When darkness fell, a dramatic effect was created by the neon-lit, fin-like tower. Inside the auditorium were 1,706 widely spaced seats, a huge screen, air-conditioning and even earpieces for the hard of hearing. The foyers and halls were wide and airy, and the auditorium was illuminated by ever-changing pastel coloured lighting. The whole effect was to emphasise a confident, comfortable future. This was the highpoint of Hollywood and the Colwyn Bay Odeon was Mecca for cinema-goers in North Wales. This was indeed one of cinema architect Harry Weedon's greatest creations. After the war the Odeon remained at the heart of the town's social life. In the nineteen fifties it staged spectacular Film Festivals. There were midnight shows, military guards of honour to greet patrons, and film

ODEON

REGD.

ODEON, COLWYN BAY

THE NAME THAT GUARANTEES PERFECT ENTERTAINMENT

The most beautiful place of Entertainment in North Wales. It is a modern building designed to hold a great number of people under ideal conditions

A very highly scientific plant is installed, enabling the atmosphere inside to be kept fresh at all times

---

Performances Daily from 2.15.   Doors open 2 p.m.

PRICES : 2/-, 1/6, 1/3, 1/- and 9d.

Tele : 2827

Acoustic aids are provided free for those whose hearing is defective

ODEON

REGD.

ALWAYS RIGHT IN THE PICTURE !

stars making celebrity appearances. Film fans would throng the railway station to greet the arrival of the stars. Sadly enthusiasm palled and crowds dwindled. Erstwhile fans began to buy television sets and attendance at cinemas across Britain declined dramatically. The Odeon's Film Festivals ended almost as soon as they had begun and on the 1st January 1957 the Colwyn Bay Odeon closed. On June 10th 1967, the building reopened as the Astra, incorporating a small cinema and a bingo hall. The Astra struggled on for a few more years before finally closing its doors for the last time on 16th October 1986. 'White Nights' was the last film ever to illuminate its silver screen. Despite some internal modifications this magnificent building had survived largely intact as a masterpiece of style and design. It was a wonderful asset to Colwyn Bay and a national treasure, and in October 1987 it was demolished.

7. Turn right along Conwy Road and first right down Marine Road, and then right again along the promenade. Ahead of you lies the pier but there used to be a little theatre (G) along here, just past the present site of the public toilets, below the railway station.

G. Catlin's Pierrot Theatre was quite an elaborate affair. There was an open-air stage, which operated only for the summer season. Opening in the early years of the twentieth century the theatre was modified and brought up to date over the years, but by the nineteen thirties was failing to pay its way. It was demolished and the site cleared. In its heyday it specialised in Pierrot Variety Shows where the entertainers wore chalky-white face make-up, loose fitting silky clown suits and pointy hats.

8. Stroll along the promenade and onto the pier (H).

H. This is indeed a pleasure pier, it was built solely as a venue for enjoyment and entertainment, with steamers calling at Rhos

pier which provided a deeper berth. Colwyn Bay's pier was opened by the famous Spanish-born soprano Adelina Patti on the 30th June 1900. Adelina also gave the inaugural concert in the magnificent end-of-pier 2,400 seat pavilion. She was accompanied by the controversial French conductor, Jules Prudence Riviere and his orchestra. Riviere had recently decamped from Llandudno in a sulk after dramatically falling out with the authorities there. Sadly his new residency was to be short-lived as he died only six months after this opening performance. The wonderful Victorian concert pavilion continued to flourish until it was destroyed by fire in 1922. In 1923 the whole pier enterprise was acquired by the Council. They introduced a two penny pier entrance charge (including use of a deckchair) to 'discourage indiscriminate lounging' and a new pavilion was built and opened on 23rd July 1923. This second Pavilion was smaller than its predecessor, but could seat an audience of 1,500. Tragically it had an even shorter life for it was utterly destroyed by fire in 1933. Another Pavilion was soon erected and opened on the 8th May 1934 but this time utility took precedence over aesthetics. Fire-resistant materials were used extensively but architectural grace was sparingly applied. This third Pavilion was altogether more modest with only 700 seats in the auditorium. Initially shows played to capacity audiences but after the war it became more difficult to fill the hall. As income fell the ravages of the sea-spray and gales took their toll. Splendour had turned into neglect and by 1968 the Council were only too pleased to sell. It was the end of an era. For almost seventy years the Pavilion had been the most important public venue in town, hosting the municipal orchestra, Mayoral Luncheons and many national conferences. The new owners were determined to transform the fading grandeur into a modern business enterprise. The Pavilion was converted into a bar and dance hall, and banks of slot machines were introduced. Success was short-lived and in 1979 a Rhyl businessman became the new owner. He went all out for naked

MEMOIR

— OF —

Mr. Harry Reynolds'

COLWYN BAY

MINSTRELS.

Composed at the request of a large number of

VISITORS and RESIDENTS of COLWYN BAY,

BY

W. LLOYD EVANS,

(THE POSTMAN POET.)

1902-1903.

May be had from the Author of "COLWYN BAY, THE QUEEN"

= One Penny. =

commercialism using the old Pavilion to stage performances by four Danish girls clad only in boots and G-string. This sad decline came to a head in 1993 when the pier was closed and the buildings boarded up. The town had once been so proud of its pier and its concert hall. Now it seemed an embarrassment, an eyesore. The Council supported demolition but a very determined individual, Mike Paxman, stepped in, bought the pier and began a long-term restoration project.

9. After viewing the pier continue along the prom, pausing after 200 yards on the site of the old Minstrels' Theatre (I).

I. At this point stood a wooden open-air theatre, with the stage facing away from the sea. There was limited deck-chair seating and unlimited standing. From 1901 Harry Reynold's Minstrels blacked-up their faces to present a show which strangely paralleled the whited faces of the Pierrots at the other end of the promenade. A modern audience would hopefully prefer the slightly surreal appeal of the Pierrots to the racist parodies of the 'Nigger Minstrels.' The most successful member of Reynold's troupe was George Elliot who went on to tour the music halls as 'The Chocolate Coloured Coon'!

10. Continue along the prom for another 200 yards, turn right and walk under the road and railway and into Colwyn Bay's pleasure garden (J). After strolling around at your leisure, exit through the main gates, turn right along Abergele Road and return to town.

J. The 47 acres of Eirias Park were acquired by the Council on April 12th, 1921 and the playing fields opened to the public in 1923. The rock-gardens were completed in 1930 and originally featured 30,000 plants of 1,500 varieties, natural cascades and rocky pools. The clay-bottomed boating lake, in the centre of the park, was opened in June 1935. Originally the boating pavilion was picturesquely thatched with Norfolk reeds. A domed bandstand was erected on the eastern shore of the boating lake and this also operated as an open air theatre. Two crown greens were laid out together with a half-timbered bowling pavilion. Model yacht racing was extremely popular in the thirties and a wonderful boating pond was built alongside a block of tennis courts. A picturesque thatched gazebo with leaded windows was provided to shelter patient parents. Together with the swings, see-saws and pitch and putt course, Eirias was a lovely place for families before the war. In season, there were firework displays every Wednesday evening, grand illuminations every night, band concerts every Sunday and even regular sheep dog trials. One Sunday in August 1938, 15,000 people were reported to have gathered to sing popular hymns to the accompaniment of the town band. On the following Bank Holiday Monday, 25,000 people were reported to be relaxing in the park, equal to the entire population of Colwyn Bay! It was a very different scene in summer 1939 when a huge number of firemen gathered here to stage a rehearsal for the expected air raids. The park echoed to the wail of air raid sirens and the simulated drone of enemy aeroplanes. High explosive bombs were ignited and huts set ablaze. During the war much of the park was dug over to provide 350 allotments but on Wednesday 15th August 1945 the crowds returned for dancing and fireworks to celebrate V.J. Day. In 1947 the park hosted the National Eisteddfod and the stone Gorsedd circle remains. Some of the profits from this event were used to commission the decorative wrought-iron gates, which you will see as you leave the park. In 1951, to mark the Festival of Britain, the Council transformed the site of the old war-time allotments into a sports arena and running track. Since then a tennis dome, a large restaurant, a dinosaur park and other facilities have been added. Despite the effects of vandalism, neglect and the A55, Eirias remains, in the words of an old guidebook, 'unquestionably one of the most beautiful municipal parks in the U.K.'

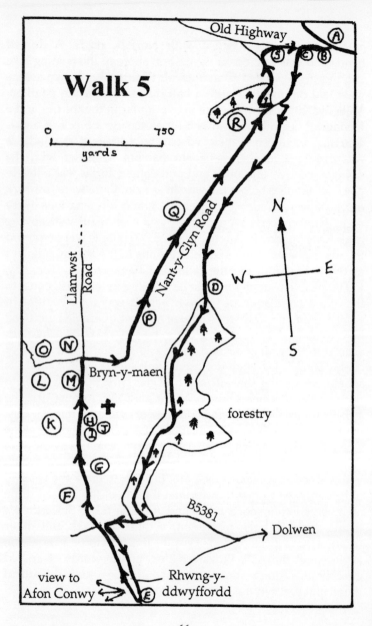

Walk 5

0 ——————— 750
yards

Old Highway

Ⓐ

Ⓢ Ⓒ Ⓑ

Ⓡ

Ⓠ

Nant-y-Glyn Road

N
W ——— E
S

Ⓓ

Ⓟ

Ⓞ Ⓝ

Llanrwst Road

Ⓛ Ⓜ

Bryn-y-maen

Ⓚ

Ⓗ Ⓘ Ⓙ

forestry

Ⓖ

Ⓕ

B5381

→ Dolwen

view to
Afon Conwy

Rhwng-y-
ddwyffordd

Ⓔ

66

Along Nant-y-Glyn to the Cathedral in the Hills

Walk Number:	Five
Distance:	Six miles
Terrain:	Gentle ascents, muddy paths and country lanes
Start:	Junction of Abergele Road and the Old Highway
Finish:	Circular route
Transport:	Centrally located
Refreshments:	Colwyn Bay only, no facilities en-route

Introduction:

Nant-y-Glyn was much loved by Victorian ramblers. One turn-of-the century guidebook describes the scenery: 'On a summer's day the lanes are redolent with honey-suckle and dog roses and although practically within the town, after a few yards the pedestrian is apparently in the depth of the country. In winter the valley is so mild and salubrious that sub-tropical plants bloom and flourish, whilst the exhalation from the profusion of shrubs of the evergreen species contributes in no small degree to give that sedative relief which the climate seems to afford to those suffering from respiratory disorders.' Combining a therapeutic stroll with a suitably Victorian tale of rags to riches, you visit the humble birthplace of Eleanor Jones before hiking along the hill-ridge to her country mansion and explore the 'Cathedral in the Hills' that Eleanor both founded and financed.

The Walk and Points of Interest:

1. From Abergele Road walk down the Old Highway (A)

A. The Old Highway was the main road through what is now Colwyn Bay until the development of a lower, coastal route in the early years of the nineteenth century.

2. Continue along this surprisingly rural lane, it soon seems we are miles from the bustle of town. The road curves to the right after about 50 yards and crosses a stream, Nant-y-Groes, with a stone building (B) alongside.

B. The small stone building is a water-pumping station built on the site of the ancient Groes Mill. This was an over-shot water-powered corn mill, which operated until the end of the nineteenth century. Like most local mills it was put out of business by the industrial steam mills whose flour was less nutritious but cheaper.

3. A few yards further on you can see an old lodge house (C) on the left.

C. This is the lodge, or gatehouse, to Nant-y-Glyn Hall which is further down the driveway (you will soon get a better view). The main house dates back to about 1867, was originally called Plas Nant-y-Glyn and may have been designed by architects Lloyd Williams & Underwood of Denbigh. The grounds have been developed as a holiday-chalet park.

4. After a few yards turn left along Nant-y-Glyn Road with the old Hall on your left. There are some attractive houses along here. About 300 yards past the Hall the road descends and is joined by a farm lane on the left. Turn sharp left and descend a footpath running alongside this lane. Soon the path

turns right; do not take the path over the first footbridge but continue and soon cross a wooden footbridge over a stream. This delightful path continues above Nant-y-Groes for 500 yards, then you reach a three-way footpath sign. Take the path which goes through the metal field gate (reinforced by a section of a French Victorian bedhead) and indicated as Ty'r Terfyn ³/₄ mile. After another 200 yards the path seems to split, take the lower course but soon bear left and ascend, following a track that leads to a metal kissing gate. Go through and continue to the scattered ruins of a farmstead (D).

D. This was Ty'r Terfyn, an eighteenth century smallholding abandoned by the end of the nineteenth century and now quite overgrown. It is overlooked by Cilgwyn Mawr on the hill above, with Cilgwyn Bach and Tal-y-bont further down this little side-valley. The sheltered location and numerous springs in this area were an attraction for the original settlers.

5. Continue past Ty'r Terfyn to the end of the path. Cross the stile on the right, turn left and find another stile across the lane. Go over this second stile and descend to the stream which you cross and then ascend the path and continue through the woodland. Unlike the varied, mature trees of the first section of the walk this is a commercial, coniferous plantation. This woodland path is easy to follow for almost a mile. You eventually cross a wooden stile onto a road. Turn right and soon turn sharp left. This section is unavoidably alongside the road so keep on the grass verge, but I think it's justified by the significance of the destination and its panoramic viewpoint. Continue south alongside Llanrwst Road for 600 yards, cross a minor junction and after 150 yards you spot a roofless stone barn (E), on the left.

E. In 1826 this old barn with its derelict and decrepit old cottage alongside comprised the isolated smallholding of Rhwngyddwyffordd which was home to William and Mary Jones and their children. In 1826 Eleanor was born, their seventh daughter. The family lived in dire poverty and the children would help out by collecting rushes, which the parents would dip and then trade as rushlight candles in exchange for bread at the village shop in Mochdre. As soon as the girls were old enough they would leave home and enter service. In 1838 Eleanor became a servant to the family of Mr James John Frost, a wealthy industrialist. Mr Frost's company manufactured cable and rope, including the rope used by Blondin in his famous 1859 walk across Niagara Falls. James Frost's son Charles was rather taken with Eleanor and on 1st September 1863 they were married in Llanddulas, Eleanor was 37 and Charles 32. They lived at Min-y-don, in Colwyn Bay but Eleanor had not forgotten her old birthplace and Charles and Eleanor were to develop great plans for the area.

6. Do admire the incredible view down into the Conwy valley from the opposite side of the road before turning and re-tracing your steps to the junction with Dolwen Road. Notice the stone school (F), down on the left.

F. This is Llwydcoed School which opened in 1880 and so wasn't available when Eleanor was young. She had to walk all the way to Llansanffraid Glan Conwy, in her wooden clogs, to attend school.

7. Continue walking north along Llanrwst Road for about 100 yards and you soon notice a farm (G) on the right with a church (I), church hall (H) and graveyard (J) beyond.

G. This is Bryn-y-maen Farm and it was bought by Charles and Eleanor to provide them with the necessary land on which to develop the new community of Bryn-y-maen. The existing tenant farmer was permitted to remain here, with the new village created a little further along the road.

H. This was built in 1895 as the first stage of Eleanor and Charles' plans for Bryn-y-maen. Initially it operated as a mission church but it was the only part of the ambitious plans that Charles was able to see carried out before his death in 1895. Later it served as a Sunday school and then a village hall. Notice the inscribed foundation stone near the foot of the porch door.

I. After Charles died in 1896 Eleanor continued with their plans and when Christ Church was completed it was dedicated to his memory, as a stone set into the church's external south wall records. The church got off to a bad start because a memorial bottle laid below the foundation stone, and containing a jubilee medal, a copy of the Times newspaper for the 3rd of May 1897, two stones from the Holy Land and a parchment setting out Eleanor's role in the church's foundation, was stolen by 'two scamps' intent on robbery. Finding no valuables, they scattered the contents and made their getaway. When finally completed two years later, the scale, quality and elevation of the building, almost 1,000 feet above sea-level, immediately led to it becoming known as, 'The Cathedral in the Hills.' The architects were Douglas and Fordham of Chester and the builder, Thomas Jones of Caernarfon. The Bishop of St Asaph performed the consecration of the church on a dull Wednesday in September 1899. Much of his address was devoted to the topic of finance and how the congregation should be as prepared to dig as deep into their pockets as their nonconformist brethren. Archdeacon Evans was rather more personal and recalled how Eleanor had been born nearby and as a child would walk to church at Llandrillo and how she had vowed if it was ever possible she would found a church near her birthplace. It was a wonderful achievement and how good it would be if they could now all work together to establish a church at, 'Llandudno Junction which was fast becoming a second Crewe'. There was an organ recital to round off the proceedings and, 'the popular hymn tune Rock of Ages displayed in fine style the splendid quality of the diapasons on the great organ.' !

J. The graveyard holds the remains of Eleanor herself (1826-1902), next to her husband in a fenced off grave situated just behind the church. When Charles was buried here there were of course no other graves, no proper church and precious little village. Nearby is the grave of John Jones who served as a church warden from 1910-1917 and lived at Cilgwyn Bach which we passed at **(D)**.

8. When you leave the churchyard cross the road and notice, ahead, the vicarage (K) and further north, Eleanor's mansion (L) with a bus stop outside (M).

K. The vicarage, dated 1898, was also paid for by Eleanor and, like the church, designed by Douglas and Fordham. The first incumbent was the Reverend Meredith Hughes.

L. This is Bryn Eglwys, the mansion Eleanor had built as her own home, which was also designed by Douglas and Fordham. Eleanor's initials and the date of completion stand above the doorway but sadly it was not long before she moved further along the road to her own final resting place in the graveyard she had created. Her plans for building further villas and developing a vital village community were never fully realised. Fortunately, her Cathedral in the Hills was completed, and remains as her lasting testament: its oak panels touchingly carved with the words, in English and Welsh, 'Father, I have glorified Thee on earth, I have finished the work which thou gavest me to do.'

M. The story of this bus stop begins in 1926, the centenary of Telford's road bridge over the Conwy. Conwy town was laying on special celebratory events and displays so Mr Hayward, the headmaster of Llwydcoed School, thought it would be nice to take the children down for a school visit. He asked Mr Owen Roberts of Tan-y-fron (a farm near the school), if he could take the children to Conwy on his lorry. Mr Roberts was agreeable and got his brother, William, to fit a couple of wooden benches and some steps onto the flat-bed lorry to add some rudimentary comfort. As word got around the children's parents and other local farmers all began asking for a trip down to Conwy. When Owen obliged he found himself being asked to organise regular Saturday trips down to the shops at the coast. So began the Bryn-y-maen to Colwyn Bay bus route! When it rained a tarpaulin was provided for passengers to shelter under a sort of ad hoc tent, with a hurricane lamp for illumination. Many relished the cosy, informal companionship of Owen Roberts' passenger lorry service. In June 1928 luxury arrived with Mr Roberts purchasing a purpose-built omnibus. In these early days you could just flag down the bus anywhere along the route and Owen would happily pick you up; for regulars he would blow his horn and wait. The service proved so popular that it wasn't long before Mr Roberts realised he needed another bus and another driver. When a chap turned up at Tan-y-fron seeking a job it seemed fortuitous until he admitted he had never actually driven a bus before. Undeterred, Owen gave him a quick introduction to the gears, brakes, clutch etc and then told him to take the bus for a run down to Pen-y-bryn, turn round and come back. Meanwhile he jumped up to watch from the hedge. As the bus reappeared from its short trip Owen threw his mac into its path as a signal for an emergency stop. An efficient squealing of the brakes and skid of the tyres ensured the driver's employment. The service expanded with Liverpool a frequent destination. Markets and fair days at Llanrwst and Abergele were especially popular with farm wives taking produce to sell. Besides eggs and butter, they carried ducks and chickens in crates and even calves in sacks, with their legs bound together and their heads sticking out the top. Those bus journeys were a real community event. One Friday in 1940, when Owen travelled to Manchester to get the customary annual renewal of his bus operator's licence it was refused, and he was told that the following Monday Crosville Motors would be taking over his service. He was out of business and his drivers had no jobs. Crosville bought his fleet for a pittance and left Owen so upset by the 'theft' of his business that he would never speak of it again, not even to his own family.

9. Now continue for a few more yards to the next house, on the corner, Bryn Awel (N), and notice an old telephone box outside the house (O) next door.

N. Bryn Awel, or Hill of the Breeze, in the thirties was the home of Owen Roberts's bus mechanic, who occasionally filled-in as a driver.

O. For many years this served as the village Post Office but now even this has closed; there is no shop, no pub and very little community. Eleanor's plans have almost come to naught.

10. Turn right here, leaving Llanrwst Road and walk down Nant-y-Glyn Road, soon passing the R.S.P.C.A. kennels on the right. The road bends to the right and soon on the left you notice Coed Teg (P).

P. Coed Teg, like the next farm you will come to, is basically early nineteenth century but, unlike Nant Ucha, this has retained much of its traditional character, especially in its attractive outbuildings.

11. Route finding is simple as we continue along Nant-y-Glyn Road. There is very little traffic along here and it really is a pleasant country lane with views along the valley and out across the bay. Pause after about 800 yards when you reach Gwern Tyno (Q) on your left.

Nant-y-Glyn

Q. Gwern Tyno is another old farmstead with its age evident in its attractive traditional outbuildings rather than its modern farmhouse.

12. After 250 metres you reach the stone gateposts of Bryn Cadno (R).

R. Bryn Cadno, also known by its anglicised name of Foxhill, served as a youth hostel for many years. The main building is a brick, terra-cotta and half-timbered creation of 1895 by Booth, Chadwick and Porter but it is set a long way down the drive and cannot be seen from here, although you may have spotted it earlier from across the valley.

13. Follow the path, which leaves the road and ascends sharply to the left after 20 metres it turns to the right, and continues alongside an old metal spear-topped fence. Follow this path as it bends left around a bungalow and after 500 metres meets Pen-y-bryn Road. Turn right here and soon you notice a footpath which descends steeply through the woods. Follow

this path for 100 yards or so until you emerge onto the Old Highway. If you turn right you will soon return to your starting point, but first notice the black and white building (S) on the right hand side of the road.

S. Sunnyside was completely rebuilt in 1875 but had previously been known as the Rising Sun, an ancient inn serving travellers along the Old Highway in the days when it was the main coach road. Robert Foulkes of the Rising Sun was an interesting local character in the nineteenth century. Combining the roles of landlord, tax collector and farrier, he was also guardian of local folklore and was a passionate lover of Welsh poetry.

Perambulating a Sedate Seaside Suburb

Walk Number:	Six
Distance:	Two miles
Terrain:	An easy, level stroll over paved surfaces
Start:	The big clock on Rhos-on-Sea Promenade
Finish:	Circular route
Transport:	Buses 12, 14, 15, 24 – approx. six per hour
Refreshments:	Good variety in Rhos-on-Sea

Introduction:

Rhos-on-Sea is a Johnny-come-lately holiday resort designed to exploit the gap between the major resorts of Llandudno and Colwyn Bay. The name was invented in 1895 by local landowner and Birmingham businessman, William Horton, who considered it more appealing to English ears, and wallets, than the historic Welsh name of Llandrillo-yn-Rhos. Retaining a modest holiday trade, Rhos is now mainly a retirement suburb by the sea, although rather an up-market suburb. Quiet tree-lined streets with individually designed villas, and small boats bobbing up and down in a beautiful bay make an ideal environment for retirement, or a peaceful afternoon stroll . . .

The Walk and Points of Interest:

1. Begin below the large clock (A) on the promenade.

A. The erection of a clock tower was originally the idea of a Mrs Bolton of Birmingham. As a child she had spent many happy holidays in Rhos-on-Sea with her parents and donated the money for a clock tower to be raised in their memory. Prior to the First World War Combermere Lodge stood on this site, surrounded by a high stone wall, but it was demolished to make way for the Llandudno to Colwyn Bay tramway.

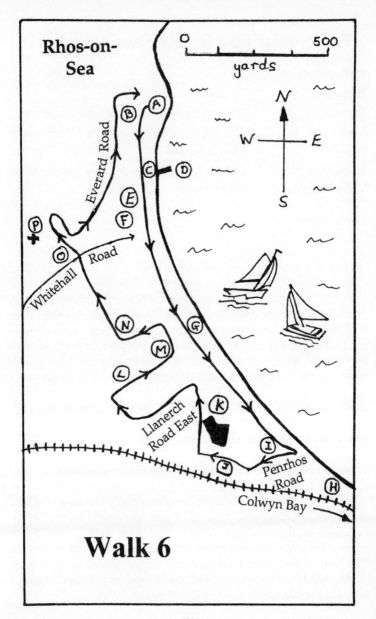

Rhos-on-Sea

0 — 500
yards

N
W — E
S

Everard Road

A
B
C
D
E
F

P

O

Whitehall Road

N

M

L

G

K

J

I

Llanerch Road East

Penrhos Road

H

Colwyn Bay

Walk 6

78

2. Notice the pub (B) across the road before continuing along the prom towards Colwyn Bay. Pause after 200 yards when you notice a large stone memorial (C) near the roadside and a slipway (D) on the seaward side. Across the road is Aberhod (E), an old white painted building with a puppet theatre (F) just to the rear.

B. The Cayley Arms was built around 1874 and replaced an old thatched house, the Rising Gull, which previously stood on this site. Initially called the Blue Bell Hotel, the present name recalls one of the old local land-owning families.

C. This monument was raised by public subscription, 'in recognition of the many public services rendered by the Rev. W. Venables Williams, M.A. Oxon, J.P., during the 31 years he was Vicar of the parish of Llandrillo-yn-Rhos.' It is unlikely that much was contributed by the farmers who unsuccessfully pleaded for relief from the Reverend's 1886 tithe demands. He responded by sending in the bailiffs, police and army to sort out the impoverished farmers. The numerous 'Gentlemen of the Road' unsympathetically committed to jail by Venables Williams J.P. probably didn't subscribe much either.

D. The slipway marks the approximate position of an old fish weir, which used to stretch out into the bay from here. These structures worked like giant, permanent nets that allowed fish to swim into them at high tide and then kept them trapped as the sea went out. A law introduced in 1861 made them illegal unless they could establish a provenance predating Magna Carta. Amazingly enough a special commission held in Conwy in 1867 accepted the legitimacy of a similar weir opposite Rhos Fynach but deemed this one too modern and it was duly destroyed.

E. Aberhod is one of the oldest buildings in Rhos and probably originates from a seventeenth century farmhouse. In the first half of the nineteenth century Aberhod still farmed 50 acres. On the 1848 tithe map where little else is indicated for Rhos, it is referred to as 'Aberhodney'. It was then owned by Whitehall Dod and occupied by William Williams.

F. The Puppet Theatre was the first one to be purpose-built in Britain when it opened in 1958. Eric Bramhall had originally introduced his puppets to Colwyn Bay in 1951 when he presented shows on a makeshift stage in Eirias Park. In 1963 the theatre hosted Britain's first International Puppet Festival.

3. Continue along the prom for another 200 yards, pausing on the unmarked site of an old Bath House (G).

G. The Bath House was a substantial two-storey building erected in the 1840's by Whitehall Dod of Bryn-dinarth and connected to it via a lane from Tan-y-bryn Road. Originally it would have been used as a sort of summerhouse, beautifully situated for entertaining and sea-bathing. Unfortunately, it was built so close to the waves that before the end of the nineteenth century its foundations had already become seriously undermined. It was demolished when the promenade from Colwyn Bay was extended.

4. Continue along the sea front for another 400 yards where you pause opposite the end of Penrhos Road. Looking towards Colwyn Bay you notice a huge block of modern red-brick flats (H) further along the promenade, on the right. Immediately opposite you, on the right-hand corner of Penrhos Road you notice Stafford House (I).

H. For more than a century the Colwyn Bay Hotel magnificently dominated the bay at this point. This 92 bedroomed palace was built in a modified chateau style, by the well known Chester architect John Douglas, and opened in October 1871. Service was exemplary and the furnishings and decoration luxurious. Adelina Patti, David Lloyd George and Cary Grant were all guests at the hotel, but sadly never shared a dinner table. During the Second World War the hotel was requisitioned and became the headquarters of the Ministry of Food. For a while after the war bookings boomed but it didn't last. As foreign travel became popular, Colwyn Bay lost its appeal and by the nineteen sixties closure was on the cards. Christmas 1973 provided the public with their last opportunity to dine at the hotel. Demolition followed in 1974. Curiously, the time and place of the hotel's original, 1871, opening also coincided with the activities of a group of born-again followers of Rebecca. Under cover of darkness and disguised as women, they chose the newly constructed stretch of promenade outside the hotel to launch the town's much resented central tollgate on its maiden voyage. Their direct-action protest proved a complete success and the tollgate was never reinstated.

I.   Gilbertville, now Stafford House, was the original home of Penrhos Girls' School. When it opened on September 23rd 1880 it was still early days for female public school education. The school was an initiative of the Wesleyan Methodist Schools Association and the first head was a Miss Wen who had come from a girls' boarding school in Norfolk. The matron was a Miss Martin and there were 12 pupils and 2 pupil-teachers. According to one early account of the school, 'Miss Martin taught piano, did much of the household management and had a wonderful way of doing hair in six-fold plaits. The visiting mathematics master was very dark and rather terrifying. The harmony master was a rather fiery person with a habit of taking snuff and the calisthenics teacher took her one hour classes once a week using wands, dumb-bells and rubber chest expanders.' The fees were 14 to 16 guineas a term including residence and 'plain school fare.' There was no set school uniform but 'plain

HOTEL
GILBERTVILLE

THE PROMENADE

PRIVATE HOTEL AND BOARDING ESTABLISHMENT

BEST POSITION IN THE BAY

SITUATED ON THE PROMENADE, DIRECTLY FACING THE SEA.   SUNNY ASPECT

Warm, well-furnished and airy Rooms. Forty Bedrooms.

HOT AND COLD RUNNING WATER

Gas or Electric Fires in most rooms.

Billiards.   Garage.   Electric Light.

Large Recreation and Dance Room. Open Fires and Central Heating.   Three Golf Links within easy reach.

Winter Residence.   Near to Penrhos College and Rydal School.

Personal attention to Visitors' comforts, particularly as to Diet.

TERMS -   -   -   3 Gns. to 5½ Gns.

Telegrams : "Gilbertville."
Telephone : 2618   R.A.C. Recommended.

Apply : MISSES HATHAWAY.

dark-coloured beaver hats' were expected to be worn in winter and 'sailor hats' in summer. Apparently the wearing of a large silver locket and chain was also 'de-rigeur.' 'A great sensation was created when two sisters appeared one Sunday in huge fawn hats with the longest of ostrich feathers and red plush dresses.' Yet the school did set high academic standards and one of the early pupils was apparently the first female to attain a degree at Sheffield University. She was subsequently, 'careful not to let strangers know that she had taken a degree or conversation would wane and she would be looked at askance as a blue stocking.'

5. Cross over and walk up Penrhos Road noticing an unusual house sited above a double garage (J). Turn right at the end of the road and, just before the footbridge, follow a lane which passes through the grounds of the old college (K).

J. Ridge Cottage is an interesting house designed by Colwyn Foulkes and described by CADW as 'a remarkable example of a small house design for its date.' Built in 1919 it combines the elements of the Neo-Georgian in a very free interpretation.

K. Penrhos College moved here in 1895 when it outgrew Gilbertville. The main building, with the half-timbered upper storey, had originally opened in 1882 as a Hydropathic Hotel. The Penrhos Governors bought the Hydro and its contents from the Pwllycrochan Estate Company. Pianos were installed in the Turkish bathroom and other treatment rooms became classrooms and studies. Over the years further conversions and extensions took place with the foundation stone for a preparatory department laid by Lloyd-George in 1910. The Penrhos girls were able to develop their own skills of public speaking through membership of the popular 'Literary and Debating Society', which was founded in 1896. Motions from those early years included; 'In time of distress it is justifiable to

COLWYN BAY HOTEL

CHESTER AND HOLYHEAD RAILWAY, NORTH WALES COAST.

This Hotel is delightfully situated on the borders of the Bay, within a few minutes' walk of Colwyn Bay Railway Station.

The Coffee Room and Ladies' Drawing Room are on the Ground Floor, overlooking the Bay and Terraces.

The Billiard and Smoke Room is also on the Ground Floor.

SEA WATER BATHS IN THE HOTEL.

The Sea Terrace belonging to the Hotel forms a fine Promenade for Visitors.

The Hotel Porters, in Scarlet Uniform, attend the Trains, and remove LUGGAGE to and from the Hotel.

STABLES, with Loose Boxes, and lock-up Coach-house, in connection with the Hotel.

Manager—MISS JONES.

EXCELLENT BATHING.

Coaches to Bettws-y-Coed, Llandudno, Great Orme's Head, viewing Conway Castle; Abergele, Marble Church, and St. Asaph, starting from and returning to the Hotel.

work for a charitable cause on Sunday?' 'Should women speak in public?' and 'This house believes all schoolgirls should wear sailor hats.' Eloquence in the French tongue was promoted by the strict application of a, 'No English at Breakfast' rule. Unsurprisingly, the provision of an alternative 'German Table' was discontinued at the outbreak of the Great War. During the Second War the College was requisitioned by the Ministry of Food, who also occupied the nearby Colwyn Bay Hotel. The school was meanwhile evacuated to Chatsworth House, in Derbyshire. In recent years there has been a reduction in the demand for boarding school places and in 1995 it was decided to amalgamate Penrhos with Rydal Boys School in Colwyn Bay. The linking of the two schools failed to sufficiently boost admissions and in 1999 Penrhos left this site and put the property up for sale.

6. Emerging onto Llannerch Road East, turn left and walk for 100 yards then turn right along Francis Avenue and right again into Bryn-y-Môr Road. Look across at number three (L) before crossing the first junction and continuing to Cayley Promenade, noticing the unusual house (M) on the left hand corner.

L. Number 3 Bryn-y-Môr Road is another architectural delight. Built in the 1930's the architect has combined the roughcast of the Arts and Crafts style with neo-Georgian windows to create an overall look of a Spanish-American mission church. Well worth seeing.

M. Moryn at 27 Cayley Promenade is an architecturally interesting, but not altogether successful, house designed in a neo-Georgian idiom by Sidney Colwyn Foulkes (1885-1971), for his own use.

7. Turn left along Cayley promenade and first left along Ebberston Road East. Pause outside the house (N) on the right hand corner of the junction with Kenelm Road.

N. Awen (Inspiration), was the home of Alvin Langdon Coburn, pioneer photographer, mystic and inventor of the Vortoscope. Although born in Massachusetts, Wales was Coburn's beloved adopted home and he spent more than half of his life here. A technical innovator, Coburn's reputation rests mainly on his talent as a photographic-artist. He was much in demand by the rich and famous and his portfolio includes studies of Holst, Sibelius, Jacob Epstein, Ezra Pound, George Bernard Shaw and H.G.Wells as well as politicians such as Theodore Roosevelt and his own personal favourite Lloyd George. His sociable personality brought him close to many of his subjects. This prompted Shaw to suggest the infamous nude study of himself posed as Rodin's The Thinker. He was a welcome guest of Lloyd George at his home in Wales and at 10 Downing Street, whilst Alvin cemented his friendship with the ageing Mark Twain by letting him win at the pool table. The editor of Picture Post believed Coburn, 'A giant amongst giants' whilst Shaw called him, 'One of the most sensitive artist-photographers now living.' He developed a mystical spirituality and enjoyed frequent journeys into the hills of Snowdonia. He felt the ancient standing stones held a special, deep mystical significance. He was also fascinated by the abstract possibilities offered by 'The Vortoscope' which he invented to take pictures through a triangular arrangement of mirrors. The results were kaleidoscopic but less highly regarded than his more conventional photographs. He lived his last nineteen years quietly in this house, surrounded by his collection of 5,000 books mostly on mysticism and Freemasonry. He died in 1966 and is buried in Llandrillo churchyard.

8. Turn right along Kenelm Road, crossing Whitehall Road continue along St George's Road, noticing the large building, Cliffe House (O), on the corner on the left, before continuing to St George's Church (P).

O. Cliffe House in Whitehall Road was the first retirement home for vegetarians in Wales, it was also the home of one of Britain's most remarkable suffragettes. Leonora Cohen, who lived until 105, shot to national fame in 1913 when she smashed a jewel case in the Tower of London in support of the militant campaign to gain votes for women.

P. St George's Church was built in 1913 and designed by the Cheltenham architect L.W. Barnard whose work on churches has been much criticised. Inside there is some nice timberwork and a fine series of memorial stained glass windows and architectural commentators tend to see St George's as an example of Barnard's work which is, 'not as bad as he often was'!

9. Retrace your steps a little, then turn left down Everard Road and right at Rhos Road to return to your starting point.

Abergele, an Old Welsh Market Town

Walk Number:	Seven
Distance:	Five miles
Terrain:	Mostly level, some muddy field paths
Start:	Pensarn railway station
Finish:	Circular route
Transport:	Hourly trains from Colwyn Bay
Refreshments:	Good variety in Abergele, two pubs in Pensarn

Introduction:

In 1800 it wasn't Llandudno, Colwyn Bay nor even Rhyl that was the Queen of the North Wales Bathing Resorts; it was Abergele. Improved roads and coach travel, and especially the French wars, all helped to direct tourists to Wales. The comparatively extensive range of facilities available in Abergele and its relative convenience for sea-bathing made the town a fashionable destination. Doctor Johnson had recorded in 1774, 'We came to Abergeley, a mean town, in which little but Welsh is spoken', but by 1824 another visitor was to observe that, 'Abergele is the resorting place of visitors from almost every county in the Kingdom; and we were informed it is difficult to find quarters for a way-laid wanderer particularly should he happen to visit this place during the bathing season.' Whilst Llandudno replaced mining with tourism and expanded rapidly, Abergele clung to its traditional role as a Welsh market town and its sea bathing role declined.

The Walk and Points of Interest:

1. Notice the station (A) before turning right over the bridge and then right again to walk along the beach (B).

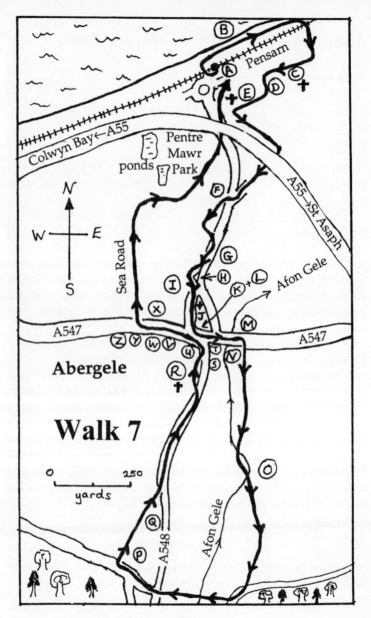

Pensarn

Colwyn Bay ←A55

Pentre
Mawr
Park

ponds

A55 →St Asaph

N

W   E

S

Sea Road

Afon Gele

Afon Gele

A547

A547

Abergele

Walk 7

0   250
yards

A. Abergele and Pensarn station opened in 1848 and rapidly developed an important goods trade. In fact more goods were handled here than at any other station between Chester and Holyhead. For passengers there was a horse drawn omnibus service, operated by the Bee Hotel, to take them into town. As the station prospered it was decided to modernise and rebuild and the previously primitive crossing was replaced by the modern road bridge. Unfortunately, Abergele had already leapt to fame as the scene of one of the most horrific railway accidents ever recorded. On the 20th August 1868, 1000 yards down the track, towards Colwyn Bay, seven wagons, including two carrying paraffin, had been temporarily allowed to halt on the main line whilst awaiting shunting operations. With no braking applied, they began to roll down the gradient in this direction. At the same time the Holyhead-bound Irish Mail roared through the station here, at sixty miles an hour. As the engine ripped into the wagons the barrels of paraffin ignited and engulfed the passenger carriages in balls of flame. Many were hideously burnt and the thirty-three who died were so effectively incinerated that little remained of their bodies.

B. This beach has also known great tragedy. On 24th August 1848, almost twenty years to the day before the rail disaster, there was an even greater loss of life by drowning. The Ocean Monarch had left Liverpool earlier in the day, bound for New York with 396 hopeful emigrants. The ship got no further than Abergele Bay where it was consumed by flames. A number of boats raced to the rescue but 178 lives were lost, with nine bodies subsequently washed ashore here. In happier times, Captain Matthew Webb used to swim from this beach whilst training for his famous 1875 cross-Channel swim.

2. After 200 yards turn right over the footbridge, past the Tennis Court Road sign, cross the road, right again and continue to the chutch (C).

The Abergele disaster

C. The Presbyterian Church was opened in 1878 to serve the English-speaking congregation that John Roberts, of Bryngwenallt, confidently expected would flock to this developing Victorian resort.

3. Continue along Marine Road for 80 metres until you reach Pen Llyn where you turn left, noticing the neglected blocks of Victorian housing (D).

D. Marine Terrace, Inkerman Terrace, Kinmel Terrace, Cambrian Terrace and South Parade were all built around 1870 in a speculative attempt to develop Abergele into a fashionable bathing resort. In 1865, and again in 1894, formal plans were submitted to the Board of Trade to erect a seaside pier at Pensarn. This would have continued the line of the first bridge you crossed over the railway and run out to sea for a distance of 920 feet. A pavilion, concert halls, shops and saloons would no doubt have been included. In 1874 the 'Abergele Visitor' observed that, 'Pensarn is a place lately built up for the convenience of sea bathers. The humble stone cottages are now overshadowed by the imposing terrace of fine houses forming South Parade...built chiefly for the accommodation of English visitors.' Bathing machines were installed on the beach and the aptly named road from the railway footbridge records the position of the numerous and popular tennis courts that were constructed to serve holidaymakers. But all was not sweetness and light. Whilst some welcomed tourism, others recognised a threat to their traditional way of life. Emrys ap Iwan fiercely opposed the building of the Presbyterian Chapel to cater for monoglot English speakers, and he scorned traders who bent over backwards to chase the Saxon pound. Local land-owners were reluctant to sell land for development and although the Kinmel Estate were involved in the erection of these few terraces, it really required a much larger commitment of land and capital to compete with the purpose-built resorts. After all, visitors to Colwyn Bay, Rhyl and Llandudno did not have to contend with tourist facilities that were a mile distant from the beach. Pensarn pier was never built, the bathing machines withdrew, caravans cover the tennis courts and the peeling decrepitude of these Victorian terraces provide eloquent testimony to the sad decline of this pioneer resort.

4. At the end of Pen Llyn, turn right along South Parade, passing a church (E) and then turning left down Queensway; continue ahead until you pass through a subway on the right and continue before crossing the main Dundonald Road and entering the park alongside a large house (F).

E. St David's Church is an architectural delight. It was erected in 1880 to compete with the Non-Conformists who had opened their English language chapel (C) 3 years earlier. Intended to be replaced later with a stone church, this 'temporary' structure originally only cost the faithful £500.

F. Pentre Mawr originated with a manor house of about 1700, which was destroyed by fire in 1850. The present building was erected in 1853 in a sort of Tudor Gothic. It was the residence of the Jones-Bateman family for many years. They also owned several hundred acres of land locally and retained their own pew in Abergele church. The house passed out of family ownership in the early years of the twentieth century when it became a girls' school before becoming the headquarters of the Abergele Urban District Council in 1935, and is now used by a housing association.

5. Turn left and follow the path along the edge of the park, leaving again after 150 yards where you turn right along Dundonald Road and notice, just ahead, the Castle Hotel (H), and across the road, a spectacular church (G).

G. St Teresa of Lisieux Roman Catholic Church is a stunning and wholly unexpected Byzantine-style church. Erected in 1934 it was the conception of an Italian immigrant architect called Rinvolucri who was living in Conwy. He went on to erect a similar church in Ludlow.

H. The Castle Hotel was only one of about twenty pubs that operated in nineteenth century Abergele. The town supported so many hostelries because of its popularity as a market place. On market and fair days the population would be swelled to several times its normal size; most would seek refreshment and many would require lodgings for a night or two. The Castle Hotel's name is a reference to a moated fourteenth century farmstead that once stood opposite in Peel Street. The name Peel itself is a reference to a sort of castle or palisaded enclosure. Only traces of the earthworks remain.

6. Turn right and continuing past Eglwys Crist and the 1863 Baptist Chapel; turn left at Groes Lwyd, noticing the Nursing Home (I) on the right, before turning right along the lane to the church (J).

I. Groes Lwyd Nursing Home was previously the old rectory. Built in 1850, it was enlarged in the 1880's by the dynamic incumbent David Evans. He was also responsible for the erection of the church at Pensarn and the Parish Rooms in Groes Lwyd.

J. The parish church of St Michael's is basically fifteenth century with later additions. The original building was erected by Elfod, Bishop of Bangor. He was the man who introduced the Roman calculation of Easter to North Wales in 768. Lewis Anwyl, vicar here in the eighteenth century, was an outspoken critic of the Anglican Church's practice of promoting well-connected English clerics over better qualified Welsh candidates. The church is usually opened on Wednesday and Friday mornings and inside there are several features worth seeking out but, before entering, notice the large stone to the left of the porch. This is an ancient penitential stone on which sinners would stand repentant, adorned in white, for the duration of divine service. Inside the church, on the north wall there are two old blocked doorways, the left hand one is referred to as the Devil's door as the excommunicated were once permitted to stand at its entrance to listen to the sermon and observe the sacraments. The parish chest is twelfth century and was carved from a single massive oak log. In the vestry some fragments of medieval stained glass are preserved in the north window, although much was smashed in the Civil War when the church was used as a barracks by the Parliamentary forces. Further evidence of this turbulent period is provided by the deeply incised grooves on the westernmost stone pillars, cut by Cromwell's troops whilst sharpening their weapons. The baptismal font was smashed, but replaced in 1663 to mark the restoration of the monarchy. Outside, in the churchyard, are three graves of particular interest. A prominent memorial stone set against the north-east wall of the graveyard marks the communal grave of the victims of the rail disaster **(A)** of 1868. Despite the minimal remains of the railway victims, they were allotted a sizeable plot for they included distinguished members of society. The poor emigrants drowned on the Ocean Monarch **(B)**, are said to be buried just to the left of the railway memorial but their grave lies unmarked and forgotten. Opposite the railway memorial and about 10 yards away lies the first Archdruid of Wales, David Griffiths (Clwydfardd), who spent his last years living with his daughter in a house on the site now occupied by the National Westminster bank.

7. Leave the churchyard and turn left down Church Street and left along Market Street, noticing Gwalia House (K) on your left before pausing outside the old Town Hall (L), with its decorative brickwork.

K. Gwalia House, presently occupied by a butcher's, used to be a tavern called the King's Head. It began life as a single-storey building but in 1883 it was decided to add an upper floor by extending the stone walls upwards, using bricks from Kinmel brickfields. When the mason, Bernard Parry, was returning from Kinmel seated on his cart, atop a load of bricks, the horse bolted and he fell beneath the wheels and was killed.

L. The Town Hall was built in 1867 by Robert Hughes, the same man who erected the large terraces at Pensarn. Just as the building of South Parade marked the apogee of ambition for Abergele as a resort, the new Town Hall marked the status of Abergele as a thriving traditional market town. Sellers brought livestock, especially cattle and horses, from all over North Wales, whilst buyers travelled here from distant parts of England. Records show that a 'beast market' operated here from at least the early fourteenth century. 'Beasts' were walked to, and from, market by drovers until railway wagons arrived in 1848. For hundreds of years stock was bought and sold along the length of Market Street where numerous traditional fairs also took place, but by 1909 motor vehicles had begun to dominate the roads. Within a couple of years the market had to be moved off the street to occupy several fields behind the main buildings. Richard Pearce ran a sales market behind the Bee Hotel, Frank Lloyd & Sons ran the Harp Market whilst the Hesketh Market was run by Jones & Beardmore. The new markets prospered but Abergele was never the same again. Yet the town continued to hold the largest horse sales in Wales. As late as the 1950's over 400 heavy horses were sometimes sold in one day, but gradually trade moved elsewhere and in 1997 the much diminished market moved to St Asaph.

8. Continue along Market Street, across the intersection with Water Street and pause on the bridge near Pen-y-bont (M), before crossing to the church (N) opposite.

M. Pen-y-bont was originally a narrow tavern stretching back along the bank of Afon Gele, but in the nineteenth century it was enlarged to incorporate the house of a plumber who lived next door. You can usually also detect the aroma of the tannery from here. Conveniently situated alongside the river, just behind the buildings on the left, it has operated in Abergele for two hundred years.

N. St Paul's Methodist Church held a grand inauguration service on 29th August 1880. All the town's shops were closed and there was much sober celebrating. Designed in a classical style by Richard Davies of Bangor, the memorial stones were laid by two local Members of Parliament, G. Osborne Morgan and John Roberts.

9. Enter the park at the rear of the church and continue alongside the river. Follow the path as it crosses and re-crosses the river and soon passes a small group of large detached houses on the left (O).

O. These houses occupy the site of Abergele's last watermill. In the early nineteenth century a windmill was also erected on the opposite bank of the river. National restrictions on the importation of corn ensured local mills like these a steady trade, but it also kept profits high for landowners and bread prices high for labourers. On April 10th 1795 four hundred Abergele residents rioted against high bread prices. When restrictions were lifted and ships began importing grain from the American prairies, huge industrial steam-powered mills were established on Merseyside. Neither windmills nor watermills could compete and both local mills have now been demolished.

10. Continue along this clearly defined path as it follows around a wooden fence and then turns right alongside the old mill race, finally crossing an open field for about 100 yards and emerging through a kissing gate onto a minor lane. From here there are panoramic views across Abergele to the bay beyond. Turn right and soon pass a curious tower house and arrive at a sort of crossroads of lanes, tracks and footpaths. You follow the left-hand footpath that disappears amidst overhanging trees. This descends for about 100 yards until you meet the most impressive obstacle you have ever seen, a fallen tree of astonishing girth. Fortunately someone has sawn just enough off for you to squeeze between the end on the right and the fence. Continue, over a metal footbridge where you next bear left around the field edge and make for the road ahead. Cross the Llanfair Road and ascend the lane almost opposite, soon turning right alongside the limestone boundary wall, along Tan-y-gopa Road. After 100 yards you notice a mysterious looking tower (P) behind the wall on the right.

P. This is part of Bryngwenallt, a mansion built for John Roberts, a prominent member of the local dynasty. The family settled here in the middle of the nineteenth century and immediately distinguished themselves as a distinctive power amongst the local landowning establishment. Where Gwrych, Kinmel and Pentre Mawr were Anglican, Tory and English, Bryngwenallt was Non-Conformist, Liberal and Welsh. However, the Roberts family was not sufficiently distinctive to eschew the ostentation of the local elite. John's original house of 1867 was enormous with a conspicuous Gothic styling. Most of it has now been demolished, including the magnificent Great Hall, but the remaining four-storey entrance tower exemplifies something of the grandeur of the original mansion.

11. Soon you turn right and descend alongside the old western boundary wall of Bryngwenallt; continue ahead until you finally walk down Lon Dawel and arrive alongside a very pretty old lodge where you turn right and pause outside Bryn Aber (Q).

Q. Bryn Aber was the birthplace of Abergele's proudest son, Robert Ambrose Jones (1851-1906), better known as Emrys ap Iwan, and this is commemorated on a plaque set into the boundary wall, alongside the road. This distinguished looking residence belies Emrys' humble origins; his father was the gardener and his mother the laundress and this was their employer's house. The family usually lived in a staff cottage but his mother was invited up to the 'big house' to make the birth

Emrys Ap Iwan

and confinement more comfortable. As he grew up Emrys was committed to learning, teaching and travel. He studied at Bala College, subsequently spending periods in Lausanne, Belgrade and Bonn before returning to North Wales where he worked fearlessly for the promotion of Welsh cultural identity, self-confidence and the rights of all small nations. He asserted the centrality of the Welsh language in Welsh politics and made history by refusing to speak English at Ruthin Magistrates' Court. Yet he was no xenophobe, he opposed all forms of servility and sought equality and mutual respect between nations and cultures. Whilst the Roberts dynasty sought to prove themselves as good as the English Establishment, Emrys took equality for granted and exhorted the Welsh to think, write and act for themselves.

12. Continue along Llanfair Road for 250 yards until you reach a large chapel (R), afterwards continuing to the George and Dragon pub (U) passing, on the opposite side of the road, the Bull Hotel (S) and then the former premises of the Ship Temperance Café (T) on the corner.

R. Mynydd Seion Chapel was completed in 1868 and was largely financed through the patronage of the Roberts family, who also paid for the erection of the schoolroom in 1887. The original 1791 chapel stands to the right of the later building. The Roberts family are commemorated by a granite monument to the front of the main chapel. For much of the nineteenth century this was the only place where local people could learn to read in their own language. One of their best-loved teachers was Thomas Lloyd, who arrived here after being evicted from his home in the village of St George for refusing to worship in the Anglican church.

S. The Bull Hotel's dining room incorporates a unique, early purpose-built Mormon Church. It was originally erected in 1849 to serve the Abergele branch of the Mormons, whose Elder was Edward Parry. A memorial plaque in the Hotel reveals more of the church's history.

T. The Ship Temperance Café (a Herb Shop at present) opened on the corner of Llanfair Road on June 1st, 1907 to provide premises where farmers and tradesmen could meet and transact business in a sober atmosphere. The project was sponsored by local Non-Conformists who had the added satisfaction of replacing a public house which had previously occupied this site.

U. In the early nineteenth century the George and Dragon was a single-storey thatched pub called the George. Curiously, the licensee was a local Methodist, Robert Pierce, who let the faithful hold their meetings here, in the yard on Sundays and in the parlour on weekdays. The George also accommodated a cooper's workshop.

13. Turn left along Market Street and continuing for 200 yards notice the following, all on your left, before pausing outside New York Cottages (Z); the Harp (V), the library (W) and the old National School (Y). Notice, also, the Bee Hotel (X), opposite the library.

V. The Harp has been a public house for at least 300 years and its interior has fortunately not yet been gutted to create one featureless room. The site previously housed the town's medieval gaol. Next door was the pharmacy of William and Mary Williams.

W. The building to the rear of Abergele Library was the scene of a dramatic protest against the Investiture of an English Royal as Prince of Wales on July 1st, 1969. George Taylor and William Jones were both well known, well liked local men, married and with young children, who began planting a bomb at around midnight. The device exploded prematurely and they were blown to pieces.

X. The travel writer, Thomas Roscoe, long ago wrote of the, 'quiet and luxury at that queen of hotels, the Bee.' In the eighteenth and early nineteenth centuries this was an important posting station with capacious stables, gardens, orchards and croquet lawns. Commercial travellers would use it as their base, 'whilst travelling abroad to ply their wares.' Before the town hall was built many of the town's public events, concerts, readings and political hustings were held in a room above the Hotel stables. In August 1868 the Coroner's Inquiry into the railway crash at Pensarn was also held here.

Y. The National School was built in 1869 mainly at the expense of Robert Bamford Hesketh of Gwrych who wished to express his support for an institution whose published aim was, 'To communicate to the poor . . . By means of a summary mode of education . . . such knowledge and habits as are sufficient to guide them through life in their proper stations . . . '

Z. New York Cottages recall the return of a successful emigrant in the first half of the nineteenth century. Having made his modest fortune in America, John Jones returned to Abergele and built these cottages to provide him with a rental income. From 1785 until 1891 a toll gate of the St Asaph Turnpike Trust blocked the main road at this point.

14. Cross over and walk along Sea Road for 400 yards before turning right into the park. Choose your own route between the ponds, tennis courts and Gorsedd circle to exit at the far right-hand corner and pass under the A55 to return to Pensarn Station.

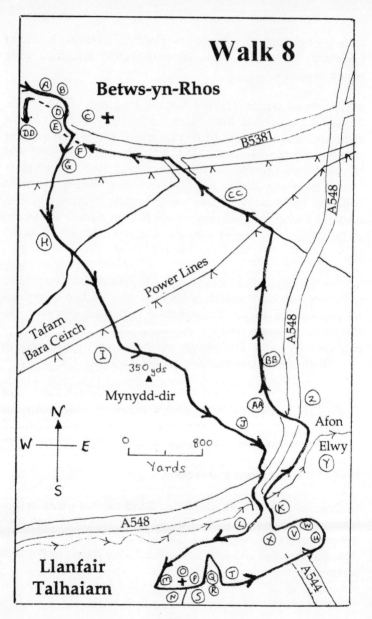

Walk 8

Betws-yn-Rhos

B5381

A548

Power Lines

Tafarn
Bara Ceirch

350 yds

Mynydd-dir

N
W — E
S

0   800
Yards

A548

Afon

Elwy

A548

A544

**Llanfair
Talhaiarn**

104

Two Villages, Several Poets and a Tragedy

Walk Number:	Eight
Distance:	Six miles
Terrain:	Quite strenuous, uphill and down dale
Start:	Betws-yn-Rhos School, Dolwen Road
Finish:	Circular route
Transport:	Bus 59 – approx. six per day
Refreshments:	Pubs in both Betws-yn-Rhos and Llanfair Talhaearn

Introduction:

Betws-yn-Rhos is a pretty little village situated a few miles inland and overlooking the bay from an elevation of about 350 feet. It lies on the old coach road that led from Chester to Holyhead by way of Denbigh, Henllan, Llannefydd, Betws-yn-Rhos, Dolwen and the Conwy Ferry. Just a couple of miles from Betws, but separated by a range of hills, nestles Llanfair Talhaearn in the picturesque Elwy valley. Over the years Llanfair Talhaearn grew into an independent, self-sufficient village community and a gathering place for poets and versifiers from the sparsely populated surrounding hills. Sadly, its most famous son, John Jones, who took the bardic name Talhaiarn, died in tragic circumstances.

The Walk and Points of Interest:

1. Starting at the school (A) notice the Vicarage (B), next door before continuing to the church (C), with the Wheatsheaf pub (D) and Tŷ Mawr (E) opposite.

A. Built in 1861 to the designs of architects Lloyd Williams and Underwood of Denbigh, this attractive building continues to serve its original function as the village school.

B. The vicarage, also 1861 and also by Lloyd Williams & Underwood has now been converted and sold as two separate private residences.

C. St Michael's Church with its curious twin towers is largely the work of architect John Welch, who employed the same novelty at Llansanffraid Glan Conwy. The Victorian improvers didn't restrict themselves here to removing ancient features; they went the whole hog, completely demolished the existing twelfth century church and in 1838 replaced it with the present building. The result is nonetheless picturesque. Internally the little balcony is charming and the 1853 church seating plan, on display in the porch, is fascinating. The assigned position of the churchgoers reflects the hierarchy of the Victorian Betws-yn-Rhos. Villagers may have been all equal in the sight of God, but obviously not in the sight of the rector. The rector here during the Civil War, the Reverend Richard Price, was an active supporter of the Royalist cause. His devotion to God was clearly not reciprocated for, in 1648, he was mortally wounded in a battle near Beaumaris.

D. The Wheatsheaf Inn began life as a thirteenth century ale house and, in the seventeenth century, became a coaching inn servicing the important Chester to Conwy traffic. Originally called the Beehive Inn, it was renamed in reference to the coat of arms of the local landowning family, the Oldfields of Ffarm.

E. Tŷ Mawr is older than its Georgian frontage may suggest; in the seventeenth century, and probably for many years previously, it served as a hospice, accommodating pilgrims. Travellers going west might be making for Ynys Enlli (Bardsey Island), where three visits was considered the sacred equivalent of one pilgrimage to Rome. Eastbound pilgrims could be heading for Holywell to become sanctified and maybe even cured in the healing waters of Saint Winifred's shrine. The buildings to the left of Tŷ Mawr, now converted for residential use, previously served as the bakehouse and stables of the hospice.

2. Continue to follow the main road as it turns to the left, past the church, notice another pub (F), on the right.

F. Llais Afon Inn was previously the Saracen's Head. Locals often referred to it as Dafarn Isaf and the Beehive, up the hill, as Dafarn Uchaf.

3. Follow the minor road that turns off to the right alongside Llais Afon, after about 50 yards you notice a chapel (G) on the left.

G. Horeb Wesleyan Methodist Chapel is one of three non-conformist chapels that flourished in Victorian Betws-yn-Rhos. Hyfrydle Calvinist Chapel in Ffordd Abergele continues and is beautifully maintained but Seion Congregational Chapel on Dolwen Road closed in 1981 and has been converted to residential use. The name Horeb is a reference to the place where God directed Moses to obtain water for his people who were in desperate need. God told Moses to smite the rock and thereupon water poured forth and his people drank and were refreshed.

4. Continuing to ascend the minor road; you are now following the old drovers' route over the hills, from Llanrwst. After about half a mile you reach a minor crossroads. Ignore the road which turns sharply to the left, as well as the road which appears to be the continuation of the one you are on (H), and opt instead for the gated farm track in between.

H. If you had continued on the drovers' road for another mile you would have arrived at the ruins of an old drovers' inn.

Originally isolated farmhouses with land to pasture the cattle overnight, these places brewed beer and offered basic board and lodging to the drovers as they escorted their bovine charges on the long journeys from home pastures to the main markets and centres of population. This particular inn, Tafarn Bara Ceirch, or the Inn of the Oatcake, didn't have a licence to sell beer so, to get around the law, they sold oatcakes and gave away the ale free of charge!

5. Go through the metal gate and continue along the lane which passes in front of Bryn Ffynnon; go through another metal field gate and turn left at the corrugated iron field-barn. Continuing along a lovely old green road, you are relieved as the path stops climbing and you begin to get views across the valleys. You continue, passing under electricity transmission wires, past Cynant Ucha, down on your left, and after another 100 yards or so you arrive at a crossroads of mountain tracks (I).

I. The track leading off to the right continues to an isolated lodge house serving the Garthewin Estate of the Wynne family. The estate owned much of the land in this area and was hugely influential. It was finally broken up and sold in 1996.

6. Go straight ahead and cross the stile located at the point where the stone wall to the right meets a metal fence, which runs away to the left. Follow the path, on the left, which runs parallel to, and just above, the long metal fence. After about 500 yards, where the path becomes rather indistinct, you head downhill towards a broken gate in the iron fence (this should be way-marked). Pass through the gate and, cutting off the bottom right hand corner of the field, pass through another metal field gate. Bear left and proceed in an easterly direction, but do not go through the gate in the extreme left hand corner of the rocky field; you want the gate about 60 yards to the right

of it which leads to a lane surfaced with roughly quarried stone. Walking down this track you soon notice a large farmstead (J) ahead.

J. Ty'n-y-ffridd is a beautiful place. The traditional range of farm outbuildings is a little neglected but full of character. The house has the look of a traditional hill farm from the rear, complete with cat-slide roof, but the front was restyled in the early nineteenth century to create a beautiful formal, Regency look. Near the rear of the farmstead, to the right of the track, is a small disused quarry.

7. Continue along the track; pass through the rusty gate and, where the farm track descends to the right, you continue ahead on a steeper course and head for the hedge-line. Crossing the lower level of the farm track you are looking for a footpath which exits the field via a stile. This path gets overgrown and may take a little searching out. Exit onto the A548, turn right and continue to Llanfair Talhaearn, which is now just 150 yards ahead. Cross the stone bridge over Afon Elwy and pause outside the Black Lion (K), with the Church Hall (L) opposite.

K. The Black Lion has been a popular tourist inn for nearly 150 years. In the Victorian period the beauty of the Elwy valley attracted coach tourists whilst the fame of the fishing captured more single-minded visitors. Efail Isa, the lower smithy, used to operate at the rear of the Black Lion but unfortunately the old smithy buildings were demolished in 1976.

L. The Church Hall was originally opened as a National school in 1836. After operating as a school for almost a century it was closed in 1929 and became a church hall.

8. Crossing to the Hall, turn left and continue along School Lane; turning right along Ffordd Tancoed you pass a children's playground on your right. Continue to the top where you turn sharp left and notice the beautiful village primary school (M).

M. Ysgol Talhaearn, erected in 1863, is full of character and architectural flourishes, such as the octagonal bell tower. The building reflects a confidence, respect and even reverence for learning and education. Modern school buildings are characterised by cheap, temporary materials, a poverty of design and aesthetics and reflect the victory of utilitarianism over deeper, more enduring values.

9. Continue past the school to the church (O) but, before reaching it, glance up the lane on the right to notice the dominating presence of the old rectory (N).

N. The size, quality and commanding position of Llanfair Talhaearn rectory all testify to the importance of the representative of the Established Church in village life in 1863 when this building was erected.

O. St Mary's Church was founded in about 450 A.D. by a wandering Celtic holy man, Talhaearn. He had been a friend of Emrys Wledig who took up the fight against the invading Saxons and was killed in battle on Rhuddlan Marshes. The story is that Talhaearn was so upset at his friend's demise that he decided to take up the Holy Life and eventually set up his cell here. Nothing of his church survives. The present building has some sixteenth century stonework and there is a legible, existing floor stone of 1623, but there is also abundant evidence of the handiwork of Victorian 'improvers'. In this case it was architect John Oldrid Scott who, in 1876, set about removing many of the earlier historic features of the church and replacing them with more fashionable features. St Mary's is fortunately usually unlocked so internal inspection should be possible. In the north-west corner of the church, concealed beneath trap doors in the floor, is a most unusual feature, a tank constructed in 1849 to provide for the baptism of adults through total immersion. It was installed to rival the popular practice offered by local Baptists whose total immersion baptisms sometimes comprised huge public open-air events in local rivers. On the north wall, notice a painting of King David playing the Welsh Harp. The Psalter in the picture is open at psalm ninety-eight, and, in translation, reads, 'Sing unto the Lord with the harp and with the voice of a psalm.' A small baize-lined recess in one of the tables in the church tells another, smaller story of Welsh social history. In the past, when the family of a deceased person was unable to meet the cost of a church funeral, it was customary to place such a table in a prominent position so that mourners might individually make a contribution to defray the churches expenses. The most famous curate who served at St Mary's is Evan Evans (1731-1789) who is better known by his bardic name of Ieuan Fardd. He is widely recognised as the greatest Celtic scholar of his day and his passion for poetry and preserving ancient literary manuscripts was equalled only by his fondness for strong drink. Both aspects of his character probably endeared him to Twm o'r Nant and he officiated at his wedding here in 1763. Twm (Thomas Edwards, 1739-1810) was a real man of the people: a poet, dramatist, comedian and political radical all rolled into one. He was famed for his 'interludes', or ad hoc dramatic performances, delivered from farm wagons or kitchen tables, which mirrored and satirised everyday life and events. Often to be found at fairs and markets, he survived between performances by working alongside the people he performed for in a succession of dead-end and arduous jobs from farm labourer to tavern-keeper. Yet these were only two of the literary characters associated with the village . . .

10. When you have looked around the inside of the church it is time to visit the churchyard (P).

P. As you leave the church look over to the left and notice a marble obelisk memorial; this marks the grave of John Jones (1810-1869), better known by his bardic name of Talhaiarn. Born and brought up in the old Harp Inn in the village (which you will visit next), Talhaiarn was nurtured in an atmosphere of popular ballads, harp playing and penillion singing, and this left a lasting impression on him. Although he trained as an architect and worked on many grand projects, including the building of the Crystal Palace in London, his heart was in poetry and song. He often worked snatches of popular songs remembered from his childhood days into his later poems. He adopted the name Talhaiarn when he was made a bard at the 1836 Bala Eisteddfod. He loved the work of Burns, and

Talhaiarn (1810-1869)

Talhaiarn's own adaptation of Tam o'Shanter is masterful. Much appreciated as a popular conductor at numerous Eisteddfodau, he was a widely known and much loved figure in nineteenth century Wales. Sadly, he became crippled with arthritis and in the 1860's had to give up his work as an architect. He returned here, to his old village home, but his affliction soon made it difficult for him even to continue writing his poetry. In dire poverty, out of desperation on August 15th 1868 he wrote to Prime Minister Benjamin Disraeli asking for an honorary pension. He explained that such a gesture would be recognised as a compliment to Wales. Disraeli turned him down. Racked with pain, penniless and unable to write, on Saturday 9th October 1869 Talhaiarn shot himself in the head. The bullet lodged in his skull but was surgically removed by Doctor Robert Davies and Talhaiarn lingered on for 8 days. Out of respect for his name everyone was reluctant to accept Talhaiarn's suicide. Incredibly, Doctor Davies proposed a verdict of 'Death from natural causes' and that was formally accepted by the inquest. There was great sadness as news of Talhaiarn's tragic death spread throughout Wales and perhaps we might understand something of how people felt from Islwyn's englynion inscribed here on his memorial: (in translation, verse one)

'Beneath the grave column you see here – there sleeps
A dear man in peace;
The author of songs and entertainments
For his country, honour to his dust.'

11. As you leave the churchyard, turn left and you will see Talhaiarn's old home (Q) in front of you, with a small bas-relief of him high up on the front.

Q. Hafod-y-gân used to be the Harp Inn, where Talhaiarn was raised in an atmosphere yet undimmed by Non-Conformist conformity. Religious disapproval of drink, dance and song had not yet strangled the popular literary and musical culture of the public house or entirely formalised its arts. This was a real, living Welsh-language arts centre with a vibrant brew of ballads and beer. In the first half of the nineteenth century, Eben Fardd, Robert ap Gwilym Ddu and Dewi Havesp would all drop in for a poem and a pint. Eben Fardd, (Ebenezer Thomas, 1802-1863) was regarded as one of Wales's foremost poets in his day. He was a bit avant-garde, stressing that literary form should be chosen to suit the content rather than just going by formal or traditional rules. Although his day job was school mastering, he was also a noted literary critic and drunk. Robert ap Gwilym Ddu, (Robert Williams, 1766-1850) was more restrained and mixed his poetic pursuits with a passion for hymn writing. Much of his work was 'kitchen sink poetry' before people had kitchen sinks, it was concerned with the everyday lives and events of his family, his friends and his neighbourhood. His Elegy on the death of his only daughter, in 1834, is recognised as one of the most moving in the Welsh language. Dewi Havesp (David Roberts, 1831-1884) was a tailor and a poet who suffered from the growing formalisation of the literary form. Although many consider him the most accomplished composer of the englyn (four line verse), form of poetry, he was criticised for reducing the artistic integrity of the englyn by his habit of composing the last line first. His own end was a pauper's death in Bala workhouse.

12. Just outside Hafod-y-gân, near the road, is a cylindrical lump of stone (R), and across the road is a workshop (S).

R. This is a most unusual mounting block designed to facilitate climbing aboard one's horse. It is probably eighteenth century and its rarity lies in the shape as mounts are typically in the form of stone steps, such as the example outside Llanrhos church.

S. This is Pen Llan Smithy (sometimes known as Efail Ucha), where the unusual fish weathervane on top of the church was made by Llew Davies. In the early nineteenth century a small private village school used to operate from these premises.

13. Turn left and descend the little pathway, taking in the views across the village. At the bottom, turn right and walk to the end of Water Street and then left along Tŷ'r Llidiart, pausing outside the three-storey building on the corner (T).

T. Siop-y-Borth used to be one of three or four butcher's shops in Llanfair Talhaearn. It was the last to survive, closing in 1985 when Mr John Edward Roberts retired.

14. Continue along Tŷ'r Llidiart, passing on the left, first Salem Chapel of 1862 and then the small, two hundred year old cottages of Morris Street. Continue across the main road and down Denbigh Road, passing the Glan Elwy sign on your right; about 50 yards further on turn left along the lane, pass an attractive old knapped flint cottage with a three storey farmhouse (U) opposite and a few yards further on.

U. Dolhaearn was originally built in the early seventeenth century but the roof was raised and an attic storey added in 1736. The occupants in those days were Evan and Mary Foulkes and their son Abel. They farmed most of the land surrounding you that has now been given over to housing. Only a 3/4 acre garden remains attached to Dolhaearn. The 1929 inscription marks a bout of inappropriate modernisation which saw the addition of the front porch, the render bands and the pebbledash. Internally many of the original heavy oak beams have, however, been retained.

15. Continue to the end of the lane, go through the field gate

and then bear left along the footpath which descends at first before climbing some rough steps to reach the main road. Continue across and walk along the footpath which soon leads out at the rear of the Swan Public House (V).

V. The Swan Inn is probably sixteenth century but owes much of its present appearance to the early nineteenth century. Like many other landlords, the licensees here used to combine their trade with a bit of smallholding. One nineteenth century licensee gave his occupation on the census as, 'landlord and pig keeper'. The triangular space outside the pub is known as Swan Square and is really the heart of the village. A troop of cavalry were mustered here in 1888 to reinforce the police and the bailiffs in their prosecution of the Denbighshire tithe wars.

16. To the right of, and slightly behind, the Swan is a white-painted three-storey house (W).

W. Gorsedd House was built on the site of a gorsedd stone raised for the village's historic Cynnant Eisteddfod. The house was erected in about 1890 by Isaac Williams to provide a home and business premises. Isaac was a cobbler and master shoe-maker and originally the ground floor bay had a proper shop-front to display his hand-made shoes and boots.

17. Look across Swan Square to the large, natural stone building, Neuadd Elwy (X), on the other side of the road.

X. This building was erected in the nineteenth century by the Wynnes of Garthewin and has a date stone on the front marking a later modernisation. In the 1800's the ground floor housed a cobbler's and a draper's shop. Over the years the building has included other public facilities, serving as a billiard hall for a while, but has latterly been sold off by the Estate and is now split into private flats. The shop next door is now the only one left operating in the village. Even the old post office, next to the Swan has closed.

18. From the Swan Inn turn right, past the former post office and the Black Lion. Cross Afon Elwy by the lovely stone bridge, turn right along the footpath by the river, and you soon reach the less attractive 1927 concrete bridge. Here you must ascend, cross the road and descend to continue your walk beside the lovely waters of the Elwy. After about 200 yards you notice the buildings of the old watermill (Y), set back on the opposite bank of the river, beyond the filter beds.

Y. The present mill buildings are about two hundred years old but there may well have been millers here on Afon Elwy for long before. During its entire working life it was owned by the Wynnes of Garthewin. The mill managed to keep going until the nineteen fifties, when it was run by George Roberts, but by then it was showing signs of age: 'It was a strange sort of Heath Robinson affair . . . all tied together with bits of string . . . everything rattled and the wheel was a very leaky contraption.' Up until the years before the second war it had been a thriving mill. Practically every farmer in the area would use the place, some making the journey from Llansannan to have their grain ground. No money would change hands; the farmers paid the miller by giving him a proportion of their grain. The old mill was sold by the Estate in the nineteen seventies and is now a private residence.

19. Continuing along the banks of Afon Elwy you reach a footbridge after a few 100 yards; do not cross but turn left and notice a very large farmstead (Z) about a quarter of a mile off across the fields to the north.

Z. This is Bron Heulog Hall, an elegant country gentleman's farmstead. Its status is well reflected in its elegant, formalised, early nineteenth century frontage, but the house itself is

117

certainly earlier. In the 1880's and 90's a small, rather unsuccessful lead mine operated on their land, just 700 yards north-east of the big house. Around the turn of the century this was the home of the Roberts family who were so affluent that their children even had their own little carriage, although admittedly it was drawn by a goat!

20. Do not make for the Hall, you need to walk on an almost westerly course, at right angles to your original direction along the riverbank. You cross the fields over a series of stiles, ascend a fairly steep bank and reach a stile alongside the main road. Cross the A548, turn left and walk south for about 15 yards before turning sharp right into a quiet country lane. Just a few yards along this lane you should notice a lovely little lodge (AA) set back on the left.

AA. This is one of the attractive lodges of the old Garthewin Estate. Notice the Strawberry-Hill-Gothic styling of the windows and the gateposts.

21. Do not follow the footpath past the lodge; it eventually leads to the route we have already travelled. Instead we will take the easier way back following the quiet country lanes. Continue along here for about 400 yards until you come to a big farmstead on your right (BB).

BB. Plas Newydd is an extremely old house. The position of the chimney against the back wall is an indication of age. It represents one of the early ways of enclosing the fireplace and its smoke instead of just having the fire in the middle of the room, and letting the smoke percolate out through the gaps in the thatched roof. A more precise indication is provided inside by a fine internal post and panel partition screen (a sort of fitted room divider), dated 1585.

22. Continue along the lane for about half a mile until it meets another lane ahead, forming a T-junction; here you turn left and after another 700 yards you notice an old farm on the right, Tŷ Celyn (CC).

CC. Tŷ Celyn is a very old house, probably sixteenth century. It is built with a timber cruck frame construction but it is unfortunately impossible to appreciate this from the outside.

23. Continue to descend the lane for another 200 yards or so, until you meet the B5381 road at a T-junction. There is another attractive old house, Nant-yr-efail, down on your right. Turn left along here and you are soon back in Betws-yn-Rhos but, before leaving, you must first walk a few yards down the minor road opposite the bus stop to take a look at Ffarm (DD).

DD. Ffarm is magnificent to behold. It is an ancient castellated house that was remodelled in 1861 by Lloyd Williams and Underwood. The Oldfield family held sway here for 171 years, beginning with Thomas who acquired the property through marriage in 1790. He was a well-known attorney who acted for the local gentry in their enclosure, or legalised theft, of Rhuddlan Marshes in 1809. He also used his best legal endeavours to ensure that paupers were not permitted to claim poor relief from the Parish of Betws. He was Clerk to the Is-Dulas Justices and before the court house was built in Abergele in 1849, the Petty Sessions were held here at Ffarm. His grandson, John Oldfield, was another legally qualified pillar of the local squirearchy. He provided beer to entertain the police and army engaged in the merciless pursuit of impoverished tenant farmers during the Tithe Wars.

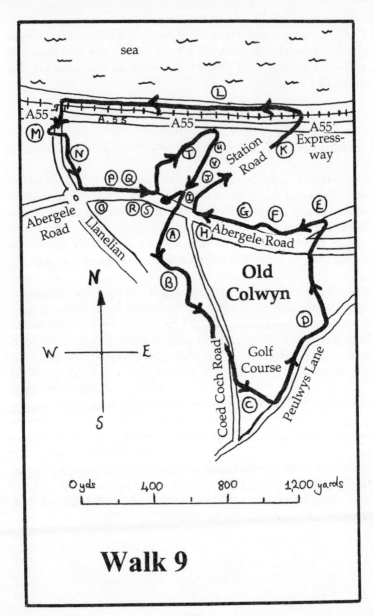

Walk 9

Strolling Around Old Colwyn

Walk Number:	Nine
Distance:	Three and a half miles
Terrain:	Excellent surfaces, little mud and gentle ascents
Start:	Junction of Abergele Road and Beach Road
Finish:	Circular route
Transport:	Buses 12, 14, 15, 22, 26, 59: approx. seven per hour
Refreshments:	Several pubs and cafes in Old Colwyn

Introduction:

Long ago eclipsed by the growth of its ambitious offspring, Old Colwyn is now passing into gentle decline. Yet there is still much to enjoy. The seafront's as bracing as ever, although the donkeys have departed. The fairies have left Fairy Glen but the stroll through their abandoned dell is a constant delight. And Mr Woodall's castellated temple of noxious indulgence once again stands resplendent.

The Walk and Points of Interest:

1. From the junction with Abergele Road walk down Beach Road and after 100 metres turn right and walk through the tunnel that passes under Abergele Road alongside the stream. Pause when you emerge on the other side in Llawr Pentre (A).

A. Llawr Pentre was the heart of the old village of Colwyn. The last house of the small terrace across the stream used to be the home of the village wheelwright, Joseph Evans. His garden was always full of wooden carts awaiting repairs. The long barn-like building on the left was a slaughterhouse, Bryn Barcut, until 1932 whilst a little further along on the left bank was an old water-powered flour mill. The mill operated here for at least two hundred years until closure in the nineteen twenties. It was demolished in the fifties and the houses of Mill Drive erected on the site.

2. Follow the path ascending on the left. At the top, bear right following the signs indicating Fairy Glen (B).

B. The delightful Fairy Glen was gifted to the people of Old Colwyn by the Coed Coch Estate in 1903. The stream flowing through this lovely little valley is the surprisingly modest Afon Colwyn.

3. Continue alongside the stream for almost half a mile until you emerge onto Coed Coch Road, which you cross; turn right and walk for 50 yards before turning left along a lane leading to the golf course (C).

C. Old Colwyn Golf Course was developed in the early years of the twentieth century by James Braid who owned the Midland Garage in Colwyn Bay (now Stermat Hardware). Initially a nine-hole course, it was expanded to eighteen holes in the nineteen thirties.

4. You are aiming for a small white gate 100 yards away, across the corner of the golf course. Through this gate you exit onto Peulwys Lane where you turn left and continue for a couple of hundred yards until you reach Peulwys Farm (D), with the farm buildings on the right and the house on the left.

D. Peulwys Farmhouse is mid-seventeenth century, although altered in 1873. During internal modernisation in the nineteen eighties, some of the original wattle and daub construction was revealed. The most interesting feature of Peulwys though is the front door. It is oak with massive iron hinges and the initials of Elizabeth and Thomas Vaughan and the date 1659 picked out in iron studs. The date is intriguing and suggests a possible connection with 'Booth's Rebellion', which followed the death of Oliver Cromwell in 1658. The forces seeking restoration rallied and, on the 7th August 1659, Sir Thomas Myddelton drew his sword in Wrexham market place and proclaimed Charles the Second lawful king. He was supported by Sir George Booth, a Cheshire baronet and four thousand of his men. They took Chester Castle without firing a shot but were soon confronted by a parliamentary army of five thousand soldiers under John Lambert, who put down the rebellion and combed North Wales for conspirators. Sir Thomas Myddleton was besieged and defeated at Chirk Castle and his estates confiscated; Captain Richard Wynn of Gwydir was captured and imprisoned in Caernarfon Castle and it is thought that a skirmish in this campaign occurred here at Peulwys Farm. The studded door may well have been a replacement for one damaged in the course of an attack. Another interesting but less dramatic feature at Peulwys was a huge old kitchen table, which served the labourers who worked here. This old table was unusual because the diners didn't get plates; instead their food was served directly into bowl-shaped depressions that had long before been carved into the thick planking of the table top. A quick scrub of the table top and that was the washing up finished! The table is fondly remembered; it was in use at at Peulwys in the nineteen twenties but its whereabouts are now unknown.

5. Turn left down the lane alongside the farmhouse and continue. Cross Llysfaen Road at the bottom, descend King's Road and cross to the nursing home (E).

E. Queen's Court Nursing Home was originally the Queen's

Hotel, built by Robert Evans in 1889 and named in honour of Victoria who had been on the throne for more than sixty years. Robert Evans was born locally but abandoned Wales and emigrated to Australia to seek his fortune. When he returned to visit his old home, he found Colwyn Bay had become a boom town so he decided to stay and try his luck here. The Queen's Hotel proved a great success with its wonderful views along the coast. It was much favoured by well-heeled visitors who prompted the creation of one of Old Colwyn's most successful and enduring businesses, Meredith and Kirkham Motors. M & K began in 1920 when Edgar Meredith used his wartime gratuity from the Indian Army to set up a business cleaning, fuelling, garaging and servicing the chauffeur-driven cars of guests staying at the Queen's. Humbler hotel guests also found the Queen's convenient as it was the terminus of the tram-route, which continued along the coast as far as Llandudno's West Shore. Unfortunately, in 1930, this end of the route was cut back, with trams terminating at Greenfield Road in Colwyn Bay. Complete closure of the whole tram system was implemented on Saturday 24th March 1956.

6. Turn left and walk along Abergele Road, continuing past the junction with Llysfaen Road but turning to the right to stroll through (or have a rest in . . .) Wynn Gardens (F), which is the small park on your right as you cross the end of Wynnstay Road.

F. This attractive little garden was given to the town in 1925 by Lieutenant-Colonel Sir R.W. Williams-Wynn, who also performed the opening ceremony.

7. As you exit the far end of Wynn Gardens you notice a church (G), in front and to the right.

G. Wynn Avenue English Methodist Church is a delight. A

stylish, arty-looking edifice, the strong, horizontal lines of the building make a refreshing break from the more common, vertical, heaven-seeking lines of typical gothic churches. It was designed by Porter and Elcock, built 1908-9 and enlarged in 1932.

8. Continue along Abergele Road for another 200 yards, and then pause at the end of Cefn Road and look across the road to the single storey M.K. building (H), before turning right into Cefn Road and pausing outside the Kwik Save supermarket (I).

H. The M.K. lock-up was originally Old Colwyn's first cinema. Opening in October 1911, it was organised and equipped by a local gymnastics instructor, Geoffrey Parry Roberts. Besides the 'perfect flicker-free pictures' there were dances on Wednesdays and a 'Physical Culture Class' on Thursdays. Always operating on a shoe-string, the cinema burnt down during the First World War in the middle of a run of William S. Hart's cowboy films.

I. The Supreme Cinema was a far more sophisticated establishment. It was opened on Saturday 3rd June 1922 by Councillor Hyde O.B.E. 'in the presence of a large and fashionable gathering.' Cllr. Hyde admitted that, 'At one time I was not especially sympathetic to picture houses, but today I must confess that I have developed the picture craze.' The moving spirit behind the enterprise and the first managing director was the well-known cinema pioneer Mr M. Saronie. The architecture was simple but attractive. The foyer was fitted with pale green wall tiles and polished French oak fittings. The main hall was decorated in Wedgewood blue and white, whilst the 600 tip-up seats were upholstered in red plush. The early silent films were accompanied by a trio of musicians playing violin, cello and piano but 1929 marked the end of an era, for on Monday, August 26th 'Talkie Week' began at the Supreme, with

George Jessel in 'Lucky Boy', an 'all talking, all singing motion picture entertainment.' The shop on the right used to sell sweets and was handy for cinema patrons, but many preferred to buy half-penny bags of monkey nuts from a grocer's on the opposite side of Cefn Road. During the war years the cinema was requisitioned and used as a government warehouse. It reopened after the war to packed houses, but declining audiences lead to closure in 1958. The building was empty for a while before being taken over by a company called Industrial Engravings. Now a supermarket, it has retained little of its former character.

9. Continue down Cefn Road, notice the Chapel opposite (J) before turning right and walking to the end of Station Road (K).

J. St John's Baptist Chapel, built in 1900, was designed by the noted Chester architect John Douglas, in partnership with C.H. Minshull.

K. This may be Station Road but there is no station, it closed on December 1st, 1952. In April 1884 the London and North West Railway opened 'Colwyn' station here, with the ticket office at this end of Station Road and the platforms above at the top of the railway embankment. Unfortunately, many passengers for Colwyn Bay alighted at this stop by mistake, so the railway company simply invented 'Old Colwyn' and renamed the station accordingly. In Victorian summer days, crowds of holidaymakers came flooding from every train but passenger numbers declined, and even before Doctor Beeching had a chance to wield his axe, the railway company closed the station. As if feeling guilty, they erased almost every trace of the old station.

10. Continue down to, and through, the passage under the A55, turn left and then walk through the old tiled subway

which survived the clearance of the railway station. Emerge with the sea in front of you, turn left and continue down the original station access path; soon you reach the end of the promenade (L).

L. This was one of the last sections of the promenade to be completed. In the early nineteenth century this spot was used as a depot for importing coal, which arrived on flat-bottomed boats. These could settle onto the beach and be unloaded at low tide. The coal was carried away by horse and cart along Beach Road, which had been specially constructed for that purpose.

11. Walk along the promenade for 500 yards and then turn left and pass under the railway and the A55. Ascend the steps to the right of the carriageway and turn left onto the footbridge (M).

M. This footbridge provides an ideal vantage point to view some of the architectural barbarism that conspires to destroy the historic gentility of Colwyn Bay. The concrete brutalism and noise of the Expressway, completed in June 1985, is an offence to the calm and serenity of the seascape beyond. The ubiquitous, towering steel lampposts are a one fingered gesture to the decorative Victorian lanterns that once served to both illuminate and grace the streets of Colwyn. The anonymous cuboid excrescence to the south-west is the North Wales Police Headquarters, which was completed in 1973.

12. Cross the bridge and continue along the footpath (N) for 200 yards until you reach Abergele Road, opposite the Marine Hotel (O).

N. This footpath is officially called the Marine Path and before Colwyn Bay was scarred by the A55 and its associated access road, this was the only route down to the sea here. To reach the

A 1934 advertisement for the Llandudno and Colwyn Bay trams beach, pedestrians originally had to take their lives into their hands and cross the railway line. One Friday afternoon in March 1911 'an old-age pensioner named John Morris' didn't quite make it. Hit by the Irish Mail train his body was cut in two and deposited between the rails, with his head several yards away. A pedestrian underpass was then installed!

O. The Marine Hotel and adjoining Marine Terrace date from about 1875. This was the first 'modern' terrace of houses to be built in Old Colwyn. In the late nineteenth century the hotel played host to an unusual event which secured the old Marine Path as a public right of way. At that time the path was part of the privately owned Glan-y-Don Estate. They were prepared to allow public access, but at a price. The story goes that Mr Roberts, a local schoolteacher, auctioned a black donkey here to raise the funds to purchase a public right of way down to the sea. Officially named the Marine Path, locals long called the route the 'Donkey Path.' In the 1920's the landlord here, Mr Robert Smallwood Parry, was granted a license to hold 'wireless concerts' on the premises.

13. Turn left and walk along Abergele Road for about a hundred yards until you reach a chapel (P), on your left with the old vicarage (Q) next door, a church (R) opposite, and the Plough Hotel (S) just a little further on. Pause at the end of Berthes Road.

P. Ebenezer Independent Chapel opened on May 4th, 1815, and is the oldest place of worship in Old Colwyn. It is worth pausing awhile in the small graveyard to reflect on the lives of some of the area's earliest residents. Notice how the gravestones record the place of residence, almost without exception, as Colwyn, rather than Old Colwyn or Colwyn Bay, as those names had not yet achieved currency. Notice too the grave of the man who rejoiced in the name of Abednego Williams, and the grave of,

'The five children of Morris and Mary Roberts who died in infancy.'

Q. St Catherine's vicarage is an attractive limestone building of 1871. It was built on land donated by Oldham Whittaker of Min-y-Don. In 1980 it was converted into flats for the elderly and renamed Llys Madoc.

R. St Catherine's Church was built in 1837 as a chapel of ease to Llandrillo-yn-Rhos Church. It became a parish church when the parish of Colwyn was created in 1844. The foundation stone was laid by Richard Butler Clough, of Min-y-Don. The east window, depicting the agony, crucifixion and ascension was donated to his memory by his widow Catherine. When the Bishop of St Asaph consecrated the church he dedicated it to St Catherine of Alexandria 'and as a mark of honour to Mrs Catherine Butler Clough who showed so much interest in the erection of the church.' Architecturally St Catherine's is interesting as a Victorian church built in a gothic style before the great Pugin-inspired revival.

S. The Plough Hotel is a lot older than it looks. Remodelled extensively in the twentieth century, the inn was originally opened in 1829. In the nineteenth century it was an important staging inn, but in the early twentieth century its stables proved more useful as a depot for Ffyfes bananas.

14. Turn left down Berthes Road and cross into Min-y-Don Park (T).

T. Min-y-Don Park was originally part of the grounds of Min-y-Don Hall, an 1830's mansion created out of a previously existing seventeenth century farmhouse by Sir Richard Butler Clough. It was Clough who developed the coal import trade that you came across earlier down on the promenade. Clough's niece, Anne Jemima, who was the founder and principal of Newnham College, Cambridge, also lived at Min-y-Don for a while. In 1911 Min-y-Don became Clive House Boys' Preparatory School, but this closed in 1937 and demolition followed in 1938. An interesting fragment of the original farm survives in the form of a converted coachhouse, now called Cwrt Bach, in Min-y-Don Road. Even before Min-y-Don's demolition, the Council had acquired some of its park-land and this was opened to the public on July 18th 1928.

15. Walk through the park on a generally north-easterly course, emerging at the end of Min-y-Don Avenue. Notice a stream a bit further on; cross over it via the footbridge and you are now in a small linear park with the stream on the right and an embankment on the left. Continue past a sort of stone grotto, on the left (U) and after 100 yards or so, notice a small 'castle' (V), up on the embankment, before regaining your original starting point.

U. This 'grotto' is one of the two wells which supplied water to the residents of Colwyn before a public piped water supply was installed in 1889. You can see the other well, nearer the stream, a little further on.

V. Tan-y-coed Tower and gardens are all that remains of the mansion house and grounds built in the 1880's for a rich Manchester businessman, Sir Charles Woodall. The noxious emissions from his habitual pipe smoking were most unwelcome in the main house so he built his own 'castle' where he could indulge in secluded contemplation. When he died in 1901 the estate changed hands, and in 1926 was purchased by Colwyn Council. They leased it to the former Welsh international footballer Johnny Neal and his wife to run as a tea garden. Opened on July 13th, 1927, the tea gardens proved a very popular facility. When the Neals left in the nineteen sixties

Tan-y-coed was besieged by vandals. In 1974 the Council demolished the main house but left the folly to suffer further dereliction. Fortunately, in 1994 the Clwyd Historic Building Trust stepped in, bought the building for £1 and spent £65,000 renovating it. It is once again a delight to all that pass this way.

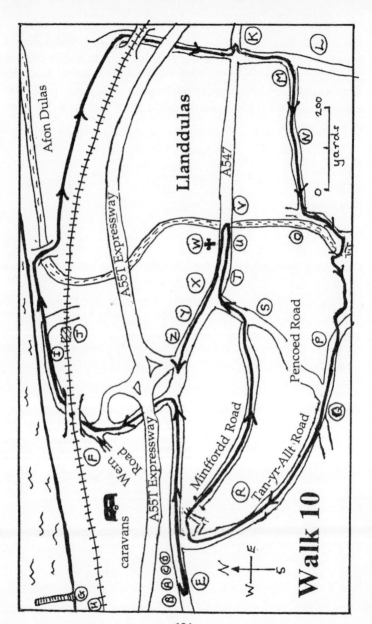

Afon Dulas

A55T Expressway

Llanddulas

A547

caravans

Wern Road

A55T Expressway

Minffordd Road

Tan-yr-Allt Road

Pencoed Road

Walk 10

yards

0   200

N
W — E
S

134

The Coastal Quarries of Llanddulas

Walk Number:	Ten
Distance:	Three miles
Terrain:	Firm, dry surfaces, some gentle ascents
Start:	Dulas Arms Hotel, Abergele Road, Llanddulas
Finish:	Circular route
Transport:	Buses 12, 14, 59: approx. five per hour
Refreshments:	Several pubs in Llanddulas

Introduction:

Quarrying made Llanddulas. It scarred the landscape and shaped the character of the people. Quarrying is hard, physical, dangerous work and the Llanddulas quarrymen sometimes required all their individual and collective strength to survive. The owners and their agents often seemed to possess hearts every bit as stony as the products of their quarries. This walk explores places, people and dramatic events from that fascinating past.

The Walk and Points of Interest:

1. From the Dulas Arms Hotel (A) notice a terrace of small houses (B) on the left and a chapel (C) on the right, with another terrace (D) alongside. Before continuing right down Abergele Road you should first cross the road for a better look at the vast quarried-out pit (E) opposite.

A. The Dulas Arms Hotel dates back to the early nineteenth century when it was known as the Dulas Arms, but from 1870 until 1944 it was called the Railway Hotel. Here the Llanddulas Silver Band used to meet for their weekly practice. Another institution close to the heart of all quarrymen also met here, the Tontine Club. This was a sort of friendly society that operated in many working class communities. Members paid in a few pence a week so they could draw benefit or pay for medical treatment in times of ill health or distress. In the quarries, accidents and injury were all too common. In January 1870 the Railway Hotel was used to hold an inquest on the death of Daniel Roberts. He had been working in a lower section of the quarry when a rock weighing about twenty pounds fell from the top of the quarry and smashed his skull.

B. This terrace of small limestone cottages is known as Tai Dulas. It was erected to house the workers when this quarry was first opened up in about 1825.

C. Caersalem Congregational Chapel was erected here in 1868 after the members had previously spent years unsuccessfully trying to obtain land in the village, such was the power of the Established Church in Llanddulas. It is now sadly redundant.

D. Pennington Terrace was erected in 1860 by the quarries to house their workers. Built on the side of the hill, these houses have two storeys at the front and three at the back. The toilets were originally at the end of the back yards. There was a piped water supply but only one tap provided to serve all ten houses. Tragedy struck here also; a past resident of number three, Mr Williams, was blinded in the quarry while Rees James of number seven was killed in a separate quarry accident. It is interesting to notice that the house at the eastern end of the terrace is bigger and joined at a right angle, this was provided for a quarry manager to emphasise his higher status.

E. This vast hole is the result of quarrying which began in the early nineteenth century. By the mid-century quarrying seems to have become the main employment for a large proportion of the Llanddulas population. Although men did the initial excavation, women and children were employed to break up the stone. The owner of the quarry in this period was John Jones who not only managed to pay low wages but also sought to avoid payment of his Poor Law Rates. However, the authorities seem to have got the money out of him in the end. Before giant machines took over, the traditional method of quarrying was to drill holes in the rock, fill them with gunpowder, ignite and blast away the rock face. This was much harder than it sounds. The driller often had to abseil down a cliff and balance on a narrow ledge. The powder sometimes exploded prematurely and quarrymen were often struck by falling rocks.

2. After descending the noisy Abergele Road for 200 yards it is a relief to turn left and walk under the flyover. Continue along Wern Road, past Bron-y-Wendon (F), and you soon reach the beach. If you look left along the shoreline you will notice a jetty (G), but can no longer see the tall industrial chimneys (H) that once stood alongside.

F. Bron-y-Wendon controlled Llanddulas. Virtually the whole village was built on Bron-y-Wendon Estate land and villagers were tenants without freehold control of their own houses or lands. The owner of the Bron-y-Wendon Estate, and much else besides, was Colonel Wynne of Garthewin. The house had been erected in 1770 as a summer residence for the Wynne family. Colonel Wynne's attitude to his tenants was much criticised. Workers' cottages were crudely built, never maintained and greatly overcrowded, with several instances of parents and up to six children sharing a bedroom. Wynne's farms were kept in similar disrepair. Where an ambitious tenant took over a run-down farm and built it up through his own endeavours and investment, then he could expect a visit from the Colonel, who would comment on the previously unrealised fecundity of the fields and promptly increase the rent. Like many other big fields and promptly increase the rent. Like many other big landowners, Wynne had previously acquired substantial portions of his estate through enclosure of the villagers' commons land.

G. Up to four jetties operated here at different periods to enable the heavy, bulky products of the quarries to be shipped to different destinations. In the 1870's, for example, sailing ships of 150-200 tons were taking limestone to Widnes for the chemical industries. By 1890 steam ships of up to about 800 tons were making deliveries to steelworks in Glasgow. When a boat arrived at a jetty the crew would wait until the tide was right before giving a signal on the ship's hooter for the quarry to begin loading. If a boat was delayed by bad weather the loaders were initially paid 'disappointment money', but eventually the quarry owners managed to save themselves money by sending the men home without payment.

H. The tall chimneys of the quarry limekilns were for many years a prominent feature of the shoreline. These were not the

Llanddulas limekilns and jetties in 1900

138

boundaries; these were huge industrial Hoffman kilns erected in about 1890. In winter the warmth of these kilns was a great attraction for tramps but if they were caught by the police, local magistrates showed little sympathy and commonly committed them to spend seven days in Rhuthun jail.

3. Turn right and, continuing along the beach, soon notice an unusual lone house on the right; this was the lifeboat house (I) and behind it, up on the railway embankment, was Llanddulas Station (J).

I. The lifeboat house opened in 1869. Over the years this proved a difficult place from which to launch a lifeboat when adverse conditions prevailed, and eventually it was decided that the superior facilities of Rhyl and Llandudno would enable them to cover this stretch of coastline more effectively. The Lifeboat Station was therefore closed in December 1932. During the station's sixty-three years commission, the Llanddulas lifeboatmen were responsible for saving 21 lives.

J. Llandddulas Railway Station operated here from July 1889 until 1st December 1952. The station was erected at the top of the embankment behind the boathouse, and the original steps up can still be seen. The wooden station building caught fire in 1913 and as the Irish Mail steamed through at speed its fine paintwork was badly scorched but the passengers were unscathed. In 1942 there was another accident when a small platform vehicle rolled onto the track and was hit by an express train. The train was largely unaffected but a porter was struck in the back by the flying debris. Fortunately he recovered later.

4. Continue along the beach, or the path, for 100 yards before crossing the little bridge over Afon Dulas. Follow the path for 800 yards, strolling onto the beach as you wish. When you reach a beachside café you turn right up Beach Road and pass

under the A55. Continue for 150 yards to the Abergele Road where you notice the wonderful gatehouse of Gwrych Castle (K).

K. This is one of the gates to Gwrych Castle which was built in 1815 by Mr Lloyd Bamford Hesketh. The main house has 125 rooms and is surrounded by 250 acres of park and woodland. The Heskeths, who also owned vast estates in Lancashire, understandably felt a little cramped at Gwrych and so had the park extended in the 1840s. Unfortunately thirty families had to be evicted from their homes to provide for the desired parkland. The Bamford Heskeths were keen to maintain their influence as well as their wealth and at election times they threatened tenants with eviction should they dare to vote against the master's candidate: a threat actually carried out by Robert Bamford Hesketh after one particular local election in 1863. Besides their enormous inherited wealth the Heskeths, as Lords of the Manor, also received royalties on every ton of stone that was shipped from Llanddulas. In the twentieth century the family seemed to have lost interest in Llanddulas and allowed Gwrych to fall into decline. It was offered to King George the Sixth as a gift but he declined to accept. Because of its dilapidated condition, when the Second World War broke out, neither the army nor the hospital authorities wanted the castle but it became a life-saver for 350 young Jews who had escaped from the Nazis. Acting as a reception centre, Gwrych gave these refugees a home until they were able to organise a new future for themselves. Aged from 14 to 17, some of the youngsters soon chose to join up and fight for the Allies, some worked on local farms, some left to train as engineers, whilst others went on to Canada or Australia. The British authorities showed little understanding of the plight of Jewish refugees; having already restricted immigration, they insisted on rounding up and imprisoning those who had escaped from Germany and Austria. The Chief Constable arrived from Colwyn Bay to carry out these instructions personally. The reception centre finally closed in 1944 and in 1946 the Estate was broken up and sold.

5. Cross Abergele Road and continue along Rhyd-y-foel Road for 100 yards. Notice the quarrying (L) that has exposed the rock on your left before pausing at the junction with Clip Terfyn, on the right, where you can see a stone boundary marker (M).

L. Quarrying began here at Cefn yr Ogof at least as early as the seventeenth century. By the nineteenth century local people felt they had a well-established right to the stone here. The Bishop of Bangor realised there was money in old rocks and instituted legal action to evict local quarryworkers in 1829. When the County Sheriff and his officials arrived to claim possession on behalf of the Bishop, they met with the opposition of 800 local people. The following day the military were called into action and they succeeded in evicting the quarrymen.

M. This Parish boundary stone is almost two hundred years old but was lost until unearthed here in 1984 during road improvements.

6. Continue down Clip Terfyn, which is a lovely lane; notice the left hand house (N) of the second set of semi's.

N. Hillside was home to a well known local family who acquired even wider fame for one particular action taken in defence of Wales. For this was the home of Lewis Valentine (1893-1986). Like his father, quarryman Samuel Valentine, Lewis was a fervent Baptist and supporter of the Welsh language, culture and nationhood. He was a founder member of Plaid Cymru in 1925 and its first parliamentary candidate in 1929. In 1936 when the Air Ministry decided to establish three new R.A.F. bombing schools at Abbotsbury in Dorset, Holy Island in

Northumberland and at Penrhos, near Pwllheli, it raised a storm of protest. Two of these sites were later considered too valuable to disturb, but the imposition of a bombing school on a small, Welsh-speaking community was deemed perfectly acceptable. The Ministry refused to review their decision or even meet a deputation. When the airfield was being built, Lewis Valentine, who was then Pastor of Tabernacle Chapel, Llandudno, along with D.J. Williams and Saunders Lewis set fire to it and then gave themselves up to the police. At the subsequent trial in Caernarfon the judge ironically stated that it was his duty to administer the laws of England and refused to allow Lewis to testify in Welsh. Despite the judge's best efforts the jury refused to convict. To ensure a less sympathetic jury, the retrial was held in London, and Lewis and his two companions were each given nine months in prison. When the trio were released in 1937, they were acclaimed by 15,000 people at the National Eisteddfod, in Caernarfon.

7. Continuing past Hillside, turn left at the chapel (O).

O. The Beulah Chapel was erected by the Calvinist Methodists in 1905 together with a caretaker's house, and all paid for by the voluntary contributions of Chapel members and their supporters. They had already established almost a century of worship in Llanddulas and this was their second purpose-built chapel in the village. It is a particularly attractive building in a beautiful setting.

8. Continue to the stile, near the bridge over the stream. Cross the stile and ascend the slope on a diagonal course to the corner of the field where you cross another stile. Continue to yet another stile and exit onto a small lane where you turn right, passing the farm gate of Llindir (P) on the right and then Arnold House (Q) on the left before descending Tan-yr-allt Road, alongside the grounds of Tan-yr-allt (R), on the right.

P. Llindir Farmhouse is a disgrace. A well-documented seventeenth century farmhouse with rare, surviving period features, it is simply being allowed to collapse. It has a stone spiral staircase and two rooms retain their original pebble flooring but the roof no longer keeps out the elements. Llindir was occupied and farmed until the middle years of the twentieth century. In the early 1900's, paying guests were also welcome but it now provides accommodation only for wildlife.

Q. Arnold House has served as a Country Club and, previously, a boys' preparatory school. There were usually around 80 boys on roll and they were 'prepared' for either Public School or the Royal Naval College at Dartmouth. When the school party made its way to Llanddulas Church for Sunday service, village children were expected to bow or curtsey to the head and his wife. The school achieved notoriety through the writings of Evelyn Waugh, who was a master here in 1925. The experience filled him with 'immeasurable gloom' and he became so depressed one night that he decided to drown himself. He went down to Llanddulas beach in the moonlight, took off his clothes and started to swim out to sea when suddenly a jellyfish heartlessly interrupted his voyage to oblivion and stung him on the shoulder. Evelyn's determination dissolved and he returned to Arnold House. Settling for a more conventional departure, 'after some valedictory discourtesies', the Head allowed him to leave before the end of term.

R. Difficult to see, but Tan-yr-allt is a mansion house built in the Elizabethan style in 1837 for John Jones, the Poor Rate evading quarry owner you met at the beginning of this walk. His workers were meanwhile housed in the slightly more modest dwellings of Tai Dulas. In the 1860's Tan-yr-allt was the home of Mr Pennington who built the other terrace you will soon see again as you descend.

9. Just before reaching the main Abergele Road, ascend a footpath on the right. Soon you cross a minor road to continue along the path before passing between some white painted bollards to emerge onto Minffordd Road, which used to be the old coach road through the village. Walk on, passing the 1846 girls' school. At the end of Minffordd notice an old lodge (S) opposite, on Pencoed Road.

S. The lodge housed the gardener employed by the big house beyond, Plas Dulas. The Plas stands in two acres of grounds and was a very attractive stone dwelling with a wonderful coach house and stabling. In the 1940's it housed an eccentric professor of Byzantine Archeology, R.M. Dawkins who toured the village in an ancient bathchair accompanied by groups of student perambulators. Plas Dulas now lies derelict and destined for demolition.

10. Turn left down Pencoed Road and right at the corner, continuing down Mill Street to the Valentine Inn (T), with the old mill buildings (U) further on, set back alongside the river.

T. The Valentine Inn is an eighteenth century house but its most interesting licensee was in occupation at the end of the nineteenth century. Named Joseph Jones, he was a real champion of the people against the powers of the local establishment. He was fearless in giving evidence to the Royal Commission on Land in Wales in 1894, despite pressure from his landlords, the Heskeths. He also fought for the poor through his role as a Poor Law Guardian. Joseph had originally taken over the licence from his sister, who had died leaving four orphaned children.

U. The present Mill House may not date from the seventeenth century but a mill certainly operated on this site in that period. Most of the non-conformist causes in Llanddulas met here in their early years before establishing their own chapels. The proximity of the water was an added attraction for the Baptists who performed at least seven baptisms in the river here.

11. Notice the building further up the hill, on the right (V) before crossing the main road to the church (W).

V. The Church House wasn't even finished before it was pressed into use in 1912 as a soup kitchen to feed quarrymen and their families, who were laid off for six weeks during the National Coal Strike. The whole village rallied round and collected more than a hundred pounds to support the families.

W. Even the name of the church is testament to the village's history of struggle for it is dedicated to St Cynbryd, a fifth century Celtic Saint said to have been murdered here by invading Saxons. The Saxons achieved physical and cultural domination. The native people called themselves Cymry but the Saxons called them 'Welsh', a word meaning foreigners, and the Saxon word predominated. Cynbryd's original sanctuary would only have been a crude shelter but we know from documentary evidence that there was a permanent church building here by the thirteenth century. That building was destroyed in 1732 by a great storm. A new church was erected but that was pulled down in 1868 as the Bamford Heskeths considered it ugly and inconvenient, and preferred to build a new one. The present building was consecrated on Monday 24th May 1869. Successive Rectors here took a very strong line in opposing the growth in nonconformity. When the first Wesleyan preacher came to Llanddulas in 1812 he was loathe to cross Afon Dulas as the rector, Thomas Parry, threatened to exercise his powers of arrest if there was any attempt to preach in his parish. In 1900 the rector, Canon Roberts, wrote to Robert Wynne demanding that he refuse to release any land for chapel building and denouncing all nonconformists as dangerous radicals.

12. Turn right on leaving the churchyard, continue past the Lewis Valentine memorial and look out for these last three features; they all lie on the right. Opposite the bus stop is a house named Daisy Nook (X); further on is the Fairview Inn (Y); and just past that, Craston House (Z). Your original starting point lies just a little further.

X. Daisy Nook was the home of another quarry victim. In 1941 Thomas Vaughan fell through a hole in the top of a lime kiln, and was incinerated. The fierce flames had been kept alight since the ovens were first ignited in the nineteenth century.

Y. The Fairview Inn was originally opened in 1889. It was here that the freehold owner of most Llanddulas, Mr Wynne of Garthewin, would come every Lady Day to extract the rents from his tenants. In the middle years of the twentieth century the Fairview provided a somewhat unusual venue for the regular worship of local Roman Catholics.

Z. The Reading Room has now closed and been converted into two houses, Tryfan and Craston House, but years ago this was an important social centre for the quarrymen. It opened in the nineteenth century with books and newspapers available to those who dropped in. Around the turn of the century it was extended and a couple of billiard tables installed. Quarrymen would book a table on the way home from work and return in the evening to play. They could also call in for a game of cards. The Reading Room occasionally served as a venue for Coroner's Inquests following accidents in the quarries. On Monday 5th December 1892 the death of Richard Jones was considered. Richard had been loading rocks into a wagon from a stack that had been brought down by explosives. The stack slipped and his leg was crushed. He was carried to the office and Doctor Morris called from Colwyn Bay. He chose to send his unqualified assistant. An hour later another messenger was sent to beg the Doctor's attendance and this time he agreed. He decided to amputate Richard's leg immediately but he didn't survive the operation. The inquest revealed that no anaesthetic had been administered and the leg had been amputated using a carpenter's saw. The jury refused to be browbeaten by the Coroner who announced that he expected them to return a conclusion of 'accidental death' and not waste any more of his time. At the resumed hearing H.M. Inspector of Factories was very critical of the lack of consideration for the men's safety at local quarries. In the previous eight years six men had been killed at Richard Jones's workplace alone. In 1893 the local newspaper also criticised the safety record of the local quarries, noting that 'Llanddulas and Llysfaen have . . . an unenviable notoriety for fatal accidents.' Sadly, little changed. The owners didn't even provide stretchers to carry the injured, and men blown apart by explosives were commonly loaded into sacks. Another inquest was held here, in September 1900, into the death of John Evans who plunged to his death when a large section of the ledge he was working from collapsed. The formal summing up made it clear that safety was still being ignored in the quarries. The owners were assiduous in their pursuit of profit, but relaxed in their provision of safe working conditions. They were getting away with murder.

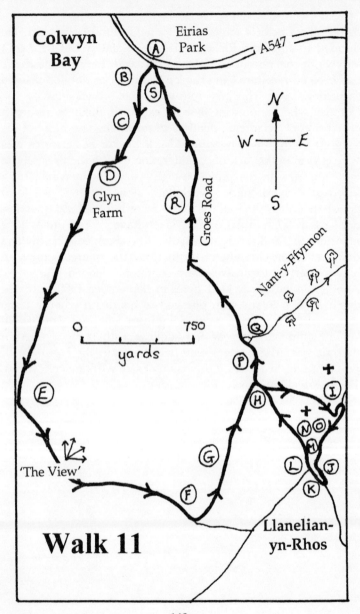

Colwyn Bay

Eirias Park

A547

Glyn Farm

Groes Road

Nant-y-Ffynnon

'The View'

Llanelian-yn-Rhos

Walk 11

0   750
yards

N
W — E
S

The Cursing Well of Llanelian

Walk Number:	Eleven
Distance:	Four miles
Terrain:	Moderately hilly, field-paths and paved lanes
Start:	The main gates of Eirias Park
Finish:	Circular
Transport:	Centrally located
Refreshments:	The White Lion pub in Llanelian is recommended

Introduction:

Water is essential for life. Springs and wells were vitally important to our early ancestors, and were rightly revered. Early Christians continued the old ways but attempted to deny the Pagan element by rededicating water sources to popular saints. They claimed that Llanelian's noted well was originally conjured forth by Saint Elian himself, in the sixth century but, whatever its origins, by the nineteenth century its exploitation was decidedly devilish.

The Walk and Points of Interest:

1. From the park entrance (A), cross the main road and walk up the ten steps at the side of a white painted house; continue along the path with Bod Alaw School (B) on the right.

A. The Groes yn Eirias Smithy stood at the entrance to what is now Eirias Park at the end of the nineteenth century. When the smithy was demolished some of the stone was reused to build the wall and gateposts at the park entrance. In the nineteenth century this was also the scene of the annual hiring fair. Farm workers would assemble here to be engaged by local farmers for the coming year.

B. Ysgol Bod Alaw, 'House of Song', might suggest a music school but this is a Welsh-medium primary school. The name has a curious derivation: the school had originally occupied the old home of the orchestral conductor, Jules Riviere, who had chosen Bod Alaw for the name of his house. The school adopted the title and, when it transferred to this site in 1972, it was decided to retain the name.

2. Continue along the footpath alongside the stream. The flow of the water has exposed fragments of old broken domestic pottery and glass (C), all along these lower levels. After about 400 yards you reach Glyn Farm (D).

C. The broken pottery remains from the days when this land was used as an official refuse tip serving Colwyn Bay. In the nineteenth and early twentieth century the council contracted-out refuse collection to anyone prepared to go round with a horse and cart and pick up people's rubbish. In its heyday, 500 cartloads of refuse were being tipped onto the fields across the stream every month.

D. Glyn Farm is a beautifully restored early seventeenth century farmhouse. In the loft there is an interesting plasterwork coat of arms bearing the date 1620 and the initials of John Vaughan, a descendant of Ednyfed Fychan.

3. Take the path to the right, in front of the farmhouse, as it passes an old cart shed on the left and then some large stone barns on the right. Walk through the farm gate and follow the path as it curves around to the left. Soon you notice a double signpost. Follow the left-hand path. You want the route indicated to Cilgwyn Mawr, 3/4 mile. You soon pass between

two massive old stones, mocked by an age which has left them stranded, with no gate to support nor field boundary to continue. Walking gently uphill you continue along a sort of ill-defined, gentle ridge with no obvious path. Do not be tempted to go through any of the gates into fields on the left. You continue in a more or less straight line in a south-westerly direction. The long corrugated metal roof of a farm outbuilding soon comes into sight and that is your next destination, Cilgwyn Mawr Farm (E). Reaching the farmyard, you cross a stile, walk across an untidy field towards the rear of the farmhouse, passing alongside a large stone barn.

E. Cilgwyn Mawr may be more than two hundred years old but shows little sign of respect for its age. The traditional outbuildings are dwarfed by unsympathetic industrial-type structures, surrounded by scrap and the farmhouse has been modernised with a similar determination to eradicate historic features. Yet there is history here for, long before the development of Colwyn Bay, this was a regular meeting place for Calvinist Methodists in the 1770's.

4. As you reach the south-west corner of the house you turn sharp left to pass just in front of the house, where you continue for 100 yards or so until you pass through the farm gate and reach a surfaced lane. You continue along this quiet lane for about ½ mile. After only 200 yards you will notice a bungalow up on the right called the View. It is not difficult to see why, for all along this lane you will enjoy stunning panoramic views. You continue until you reach a single storey house called Tyn-y-coed (F), on the left.

F. Tyn-y-coed has been much modernised but there has been a house here for at least 250 years. The Calvinist Methodists met here after moving from Cilgwyn Mawr and before acquiring their own chapel. At this stage they had grown to a membership of twenty-four.

5. Turn left and follow the footpath, which runs alongside Tyn-y-coed. Keeping the stream on your right you continue for 400 yards until you reach a spot where another little stream comes in from the left. Here you descend to cross a little wooden bridge and then ascend the bank to almost immediately arrive outside Meifod (G).

G. Meifod is probably seventeenth century, although the outbuildings have retained their character far better than the house. In 1751 it was the home of the rector of Llanelian Church, the Reverend Lewis Lloyd, who also ran a village school educating about 30 pupils. The farm takes its name from the stream, Nant Meifod, which makes this dingle such a delightful spot.

6. Continue along the path past the farm and above and alongside the stream. After about a 100 yards you reach a surfaced lane. Turn right and ascend this lane, past New York Cottage (H), on the right. Within a few yards you notice a footpath sign on your left. Cross the stile and keeping to the left of the hedge follow it around, finally exiting at the far right hand corner of the second field onto an unpaved lane. When this short lane meets a road, turn left and continue along the road for 150 yards until you reach a chapel (I), on your left.

H. New York Cottage used to have a neighbouring cottage, Pen-yr-allt, situated a little higher-up, on the opposite side of the road. The ruins of Pen-yr-allt remain amongst the dense vegetation. Here, in 1897, the residents of both cottages were involved in the sensational death of 9 year old Annie Hughes. Abigail Roberts of New York Cottage was the main witness whilst the victim's own mother, Mary Ellen Hughes of Pen-yr-allt, was accused of killing Annie by fracturing the child's skull with a rock. The child's father, Robert Hughes, seemed determined to place all blame for their daughter's death on his wife, Mary. The truth seemed to be that Mary was almost as much a victim as Annie, for Robert was a drunken, violent bully who had come in from the pub, attacked his wife, kicking and punching her until her eyes and shins were blackened. Mary had picked up a stone from near the cottage door intending to defend herself from her advancing husband. Whereupon little Annie had intervened to defend her mother, crying, 'Daddy don't!' and had been tragically struck by a blow intended for Robert. Fortunately, Abigail Roberts's testimony supported Mary and she was eventually acquitted.

I. Llanelian Ebenezer Baptist Chapel and its grounds have maintained their beautiful simplicity. The setting, overlooking the bay, is fine and the monuments neatly preserved. The stone protected by black gothic railings commemorates a Victorian resident of the farm we have just visited, John Hughes, of Meifod, who died on the 2nd February 1865 aged only 36. He was joined by his wife Jane and his infant son, only two years later. A memorial stone set into the front of the chapel sets out the following brief chronology, in Welsh; Built 1831, Enlarged 1840 and Renovated 1887.

7. Leaving the Chapel, return to the point at which you first met this road. The building to the left may call itself Hen Efail, but it is neither. The old smithy was demolished and replaced by the present dwelling, which is otherwise devoid of historic interest. Continue walking alongside the road; soon you notice the village church ahead. Follow the road as it first turns left and then right. At the crossroads in the centre of Llanelian, first turn left and walk a few yards until you notice a building (J) with a red Post Office letter box set into its boundary wall. Opposite is Llan Farmhouse (K), with a thatched roof.

J. The right hand side of this semi-detached building used to operate as the village Post Office, but no more. The chimneys of this building are a particularly interesting feature and a clue to its origins for few ordinary customers would be prepared to pay so much extra for such fancy chimneys. These were built as estate cottages for Coed Coch and were given such flourishes to reflect the wealth and taste of the Estate owner rather than that of the humble occupants.

K. Llan Farm is a medieval cruck house whose outer walls were rebuilt in stone in the late fifteenth century. Internally there is still some remaining wattle and daub walling, especially under the stairs. The original five crucks all still remain, at least in part. Some of the timber framing can be seen externally in the gable end. In Victorian times this was the home of the sexton, Jabez Jones.

8. Turn right, take a few paces, and then pause outside the unpainted stone building (L).

L. Now completely rebuilt, this was originally the main village smithy. Notice the initials of the Coed Coch Estate on the date board on the front of the building.

9. Turn around and walk back across the car park, stopping in front of the pub (M), with the church (N) and its graveyard (O) beyond.

M. The White Lion Inn may seem to occupy an anomalous position alongside the church but this was previously a common and eminently sensible arrangement. Worshippers often had to travel long distances on foot or horseback to attend church, and the services of a conveniently placed hostelry were much appreciated. The Victorian insistence on sobriety led to many such fine old inns being demolished, such as the Mostyn Arms and the Queen's Head at Llanrhos, and the re-siting of the Ship at Llandrillo-yn-Rhos. Towards the end of the eighteenth century the licensee here, John Parry, became quite a famous bard. In previous days the inn also acted as a temporary Estate Office for the agent of the Coed Coch Estate who would attend every half-year for tenants to call in and pay their farm rents. The White Lion has been sympathetically restored and retains much character both inside and out.

N. St Elian's Church was founded here with a wooden or wattle

An artists impression of St. Elian's well

and daub building in about 540 A.D. Its later stone replacement, which we see here, has suffered like many other churches from over-enthusiastic Victorian restoration, in this case in 1859. Inside, the nine wooden Tudor panels depicting the Last Judgement, the Ascension and the legend of St Hubert are interesting and rare. The north chapel is thought to be ninth century whilst the carved head above the entrance is supposed to represent St Elian.

O. The grave of the White Lion's licensee-bard, John Parry, 1770-1820 is to be found where the little path in front of the church bends to the left. Parry was well known for his lively wit and repartee, but his most highly regarded work was the poem, Myfyrdod Mewn Mynwent which is commonly compared to Gray's Elegy. At the rear of the church can be found the grave of one of the past owners of the Coed Coch Estate, John Lloyd Wynne 1776-1862.

10. Leave the churchyard as you entered, and then walk along the road which passes behind the White Lion and in front of the Smithy, passing another house displaying the CC of Coed Coch on the left. This narrow lane is actually Groes Road and you follow it all the way back to Colwyn Bay, as it carries very little traffic and retains much of the character of an old country lane. After 300 yards you are back at the place where you left the lane from Meifod. Just a few yards further takes you to an old chapel (P).

P. Nant y Ffynnon Chapel opened on the 25th May 1833 as the meeting place of the Calvinist Methodists who had previously wandered from Cilgwyn Mawr to Tyn-y-coed. The builder was David Williams of Frongoch, Llansanffraid. The chapel had an average membership of only about 30 but still managed to raise enough money to install a new harmonium in 1899 and in 1907 they raised a further £170 for modernisation of the building. A seemingly inevitable decline in membership led to closure in 1994.

11. Continuing for about 100 yards, the road bends left and you should stop, half way along before it turns right again. Down on your right, now hidden amongst the undergrowth is a spot once infamous throughout Wales, Ffynnon Elian (Q).

Q. Ffynnon Elian was once revered as a magical place. Before being deliberately destroyed it comprised a circular well with an arched stone roof, covered in turf, surrounded by a strong square stone wall and with a cobbled pathway leading down to it from the roadside. Its story really begins 1,500 years ago when St Elian was strolling along here. He began to feel rather ill and desperately in need of some cooling water. He knelt and prayed for relief, when suddenly a spring gushed forth. The waters seem to magically soothe and heal his fever. The word got round and soon pilgrims were travelling miles to seek help and relief from their afflictions. Unfortunately some pilgrims prayed rather less for the removal of their own afflictions than the imposition of afflictions on others. Before long St Elian's well became more famous for the efficacy of its curses rather than its cures! A whole industry sprang up around this famed cursing well. Local people sometimes professed expertise in helping visitors exploit the cursing potential of the well, in return for a modest fee. A sort of ritual developed whereby the curser would be advised by the 'priest' to write the name of the intended victim on a pebble, hold it tightly and stand alongside the well. Meanwhile the 'priest' would intone passages from scripture before dipping a container into the water. The curser would be invited to drink from the container and cast the dregs over their shoulder. This was repeated three times, each time the curser would assert their evil wishes, finally dropping the pebble bearing the name of the soon to be afflicted into the well. In the early years of the nineteenth century the standard charge for assisting in this venomous activity was a shilling to help apply a curse and ten shillings to assist in revoking a curse. Whilst the ancient Celts were happy to celebrate the power and importance of sacred wells, it had long fallen out of favour with both the Established Church and the Nonconformists who began to regard this as at best pagan, and at worst a criminal con-trick. In 1818 the authorities sent John Edwards to prison for a year for exploiting intended cursers, although the actual charge was 'obtaining money under false pretences'. In 1823 John Evans, better known as Jac Ffynon Elian, was gaoled for similar activities. Even after the Rector did his best to completely obliterate the well in January 1829, the cursing continued and in 1831 Jac Ffynon Elian was gaoled again for a repeat offence. In 1845 'hundreds of people every year' were still coming to curse, but by the end of the century the old custom seemed to have ended, although the physical remains of the well could still be discerned. Now we must just pause and imagine . . .

12. Continue to descend Groes Road (R) for about ¾ mile, pausing outside Colwyn Bay Motorcycles (S), before regaining your original starting position outside Eirias Park.

R. Groes Road is an ancient thoroughfare and may have originally got its name from a roadside cross. There is no written evidence for this but there were certainly stocks sited at the end where Groes Road meets Abergele Road because in 1777 the parish paid £1 for a new set to be installed there.

S. The Colwyn Bay Laundry originally occupied the buildings now used by Colwyn Bay Motorcycles. The opening of the laundry in June 1900 was commemorated with a celebratory dinner at the Queen's Hotel, Old Colwyn. Mr Thomas Barnard, the owner's son, claimed in his speech that, 'Every good housewife now saw that it was to her advantage to send the family wash to a laundry. When the husband returned home on

the evening of washing day he no longer had his temper ruffled by the steam and the sight of clothes drying before the fire, but found his home on that day as on other days, cheerful, bright and happy.' The laundry employed about fifty people, nearly all of whom were women, although it is dubious whether their work was as 'light and enjoyable' as the proprietor claimed. To allay the widespread fears that steam laundries were unnatural and that the machinery would tear the washing, potential customers were invited to, 'Peep behind the scenes and see the laundry in action.' Over the years as the number of holidaymakers staying in Colwyn Bay declined and the availability and efficiency of domestic washing machines increased, the demand for the laundry's services shrunk dramatically and its demise became inevitable.

Scandal at Congo House

Walk Number:	Twelve
Distance:	Two miles
Terrain:	A town trail along good, fairly level surfaces
Start:	Rosemary Avenue, Colwyn Bay
Finish:	Old Colwyn Cemetery, Llanelian Road
Transport:	Buses 22, 59 for return: approx. two per hour
Refreshments:	Good variety in Old Colwyn and Colwyn Bay

Introduction:

'The African Children, walking in the streets of Colwyn Bay have now become a feature of the place' observed Heywood's 1892 holiday guidebook. The Africans lived and studied in Colwyn Bay at Congo House, which displays no mark of its former significance. William Hughes, the inspiration, founder and director of this pioneering venture in Black education, has long been forgotten by the town. Yet both students and director lie buried here, and many places remain to echo a fascinating tale which made national headlines in 1911.

The Walk and Points of Interest:

1. Begin outside Myrtle Villa, the large detached building (A) on the corner of Rosemary Avenue and Nant-y-glyn Road.

A. Myrtle Villa is now the 'Glyn Colwyn Office' of Conwy Social Services department, but in 1890 it was the Congo House Training Institute. The Congo House Institute was founded by the Reverend William Hughes, who had previously worked in

161

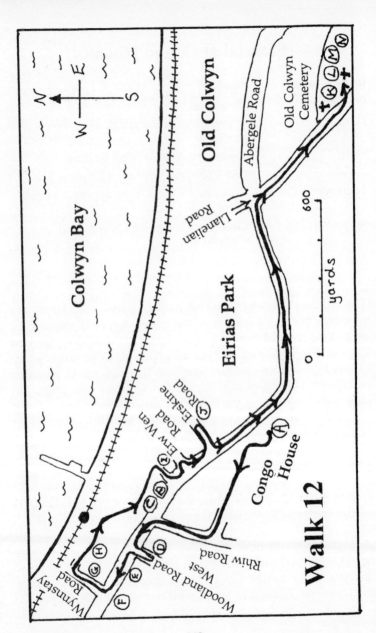

Walk 12

Colwyn Bay

Old Colwyn

Eirias Park

Congo House

Abergele Road

Old Colwyn Cemetery

Llanelian Road

Erskine Road

Erw Wen Road

Woodland Road West

Rhiw Road

Wynnstay Road

yards
0   600

A B C D E F G H I J K L M N

Africa as a Baptist missionary. During his years in the Congo he had been shocked by the arrogance of other missionaries who treated the beliefs and sacred objects of the native peoples with contempt. He believed people should be led to Christ, not dragged. William Hughes was not completely free from cultural bias but he regarded black people as the equal of whites in an age when even supposedly educated whites were appallingly racist. As late as 1911 the Encyclopaedia Britannica claimed, 'The Negro . . . would appear to stand on a lower evolutionary plane to the white man, and to be more closely related to the anthropoids.' William was born in 1855 near Criccieth, trained at Llangollen Baptist College and sailed in 1882 for the Congo. After three years in Africa, William became disenchanted with the traditional role of the white missionary. He became convinced that any proselytising of Africa would be better done by Africans themselves, particularly if they could offer their people useful, practical skills as well as pearls of wisdom from the Bible. He decided to set-up such a scheme and when he returned to North Wales in 1885 he was accompanied by his first two black students, Kinkasa and Nkanza. Initially they visited Baptist Chapels throughout Wales and the North of England speaking, singing and selling little photographs of the boys to raise funds and support for the proposed institute. At the beginning of 1890 their efforts came to fruition with the opening of their institute in this impressive building.

2. Descend Nant-y-glyn Road, turning first left along Nant-y-glyn Avenue; continue along Park Road, then turn right down Rhiw Road to the bottom. Look right, and across the road you will notice Tabernacl Chapel (B) and the Public Hall (C).

B. Tabernacl Baptist Chapel was founded by Rev. William Hughes in 1888. He served at the Welsh Baptist Chapels in Llanelian and Old Colwyn in 1887 whilst he helped establish the cause here in Colwyn Bay. By 1892 he was too busy at Congo

House to also be in charge here so the Reverend Evans took over as minister. The chapel continued its links with Congo House as both students and staff regularly attended here.

C. The Public Hall provided a public face for the Institute. In the summer, advertisements were placed in local newspapers inviting residents and visitors to services which included talks from students, staff and distinguished visiting speakers. In 1895 the anti-colonial Nigerian Church leader, Mojola Agbebi spoke here in support of the work of William Hughes and the Institute. But it wasn't all serious, entertaining events and exhibitions were frequently held both here and in the grounds of the institute itself. The Congo Institute offered the Colwyn Bay public an insight into Black culture and tradition far removed from the racist parodies of the 'Nigger Minstrels' on the promenade.

3. Turn left and continuing along Abergele Road firstly visit the foyer of the library (D), just up Woodland Road West, on your left, then notice Bradford House (E), (the florists next to H.S.B.C.) before halting at Crown Buildings (F), opposite the end of Wynnstay Road.

D. The library has a brass memorial plaque on the wall, on the right, just inside the entrance. At the bottom is inscribed the name of the Reverend William Hughes F.R.G.S. for he was one of the prime movers in the scheme to provide this wonderful library for the people of Colwyn Bay. The F.R.G.S. is a reference to his having been elected a Fellow of the Royal Geographical Society, having been proposed by his friend and supporter, the famous explorer H.M. Stanley. The opening ceremony was performed by the Reverend Thomas Parry, J.P. who was another long-term supporter of Congo House.

E. Bradford House, on Conwy Road used to be 'Lewis Brothers Tailors.' At the turn of the century Etim, Richard, and Joseph Burnley were three of the Congo House students who served their apprenticeship here.

F. Crown Buildings replaced the old Council buildings where, for six years, Rev. William Hughes attended meetings as a Councillor. William constantly involved himself with good causes and was also an acclaimed Secretary of the 1910 National Eisteddfod. Towards the end of his Council service criticisms began to surface in Colwyn Bay concerning his running of Congo House. After attending the Council Meeting on 4th January 1912 he was never to return; his whole world was collapsing around him . . .

4. Cross the main road and pause outside the offices of Gwynfor Jones & Co. (G), on Wynnstay Road.

G. For many years this was Preswylfa, the local office of the Conwy Union, the body responsible for the operations of the Workhouse and the Poor Law. As the storm clouds gathered around William, it became clear that he might fall so far from grace that he could end in their clutches . . .

5. Continue to the end of Wynnstay Road, turn right along Prince's Drive and pause outside the old Metropole Hotel (H), on the corner of Penrhyn Road.

H. On Thursday 4th July, 1912, at the Hotel Metropole, the curtain came down on the Congo House Institute. It was destroyed by a front page story in a national news magazine, John Bull. Under the headlines, 'A BAPTIST MISSION SCANDAL – RICH LADIES AND "CONVERTED" NEGROES the magazine tore into the character of Reverend Hughes, his use of the Institute's finances and the sexual conduct of the students. This was followed by another article the following week. The previous stream of voluntary contributions to Congo House dried up immediately, and tradesmen with outstanding bills got nervous and demanded immediate payment. Unless William could prove libel, all would be lost. On Wednesday 12th June 1912 at Denbighshire Assizes in Rhuthun, before Mr Justice Lush and a specially sworn-in jury, the Reverend William Hughes began libel proceedings against the publishers of John Bull. It transpired that John Bull had sent an undercover reporter to a Bible study session at the Institute to see if he could add any lurid details to its already formed character assassination story. It also transpired, although it was never made clear to the jury, that the visiting black student referred to in the subsequent magazine article was also a plant by the magazine. He had actually been expelled by the Institute years before and had 'coincidentally' chosen to return for a visit at the very same session as that attended by the undercover reporter. Unlike John Bull's proprietor Horatio Bottomley, who appeared

in person at the trial, William made an appallingly bad witness. It was clear that after the enthusiasm of the Institute's early days it had become harder to attract sufficient funds. Having invested his whole personality, as well as his entire life savings, in the enterprise William could not bear to admit failure and was driven to more and more dubious practices to keep up the appearance of financial viability. He issued at least 20 cheques knowing there were no funds to support them and he exaggerated the numbers and achievements of his students to boost the prestige of the Institute and attract more subscribers. Yet unlike his detractors William Hughes was sincere. He was motivated by the wish to serve Africa and had a profound respect for Black Africans. John Bull and many of his other critics were motivated by racism and petty self-interest. He lost the libel case, his beloved Institute and many of his friends. Yet William did not completely abandon his mission . . .

SALE ON WEDNESDAY NEXT.

By Order of the Liquidator.

COLWYN BAY.

HIGHLY IMPORTANT SALE of the Valuable FREEHOLD PROPERTY known as MYRTLE VILLA and THE AFRICAN INSTITUTE, with the Valuable BUILDING LAND adjoining.

MR. F. A. DEW is favoured with instructions from J. H. Jones, Esq., of Llandudno, the Liquidator, to Sell by Auction at the Hotel Metropole, Colwyn Bay, on Wednesday, 31st July, 1912, at 3.30 p.m. (subject to Conditions of Sale), the beautifully situated and highly valuable

FREEHOLD PROPERTY.
known as
THE AFRICAN INSTITUTE,
MYRTLE VILLA,
and the
BUILDING LAND ADJOINING
THE SAME,

which is ripe for immediate development. The Property will first be offered in one Lot, and if not so sold, then in Lots as shewn in Particulars of Sale and Plan.

Plans, Particulars of Sale, and further information may be obtained from J. H. Jones, Esq., Accountant, Grange House Llandudno; Messrs. J. M. Porter & Elcock, Surveyors, Colwyn Bay; Mr. F. A. Dew, Auctioneer and Estate Agent, The Property Mart, Colwyn Bay; or from

Messrs. CHAMBERLAIN & JOHNSON,
Solicitors,
Llandudno.

---

6. Continue along Sea View Road, first left along Bay View Road, right along Greenfield Road, left along Abergele Road, pausing on the corner of Erw Wen Road to notice Powlson's printers (I) before proceeding to the second turning on the left, Erskine Road to notice number 22, Gwylfa (J).

I. Powlson Printers have been in Colwyn Bay since Victorian times and in the early, happy days at the Institute was one of the local firms who provided apprenticeships for African students. Nkanza, Paul and Osata were all trained here.

J. Gwylfa continues the story of what happened to William after the scandal. This was the home of Azariah Jones who continued to support William through thick and thin. William still clung to the ideals of the African Institute and continued to include the name as the heading on his correspondence. He decided to once again take up his mission in Africa. The idea was to work with Pastor Alfred Dibundu, an old boy of the Colwyn Bay Institute, in Duala in the Cameroons. William was to be provided with a wooden house and a small income but needed further funds to provide a decent income and pay for his passage. Azariah Jones acted as treasurer to receive financial contributions for this Cameroons scheme. The First World War and the German invasion of the Cameroons caused delays, but anticipating his imminent departure in 1917, many old friends got together to present William with an illuminated address. This set out the many aspects of his contribution to the life of Colwyn Bay and offered admiration and thanks. Departure was delayed again. In 1918 funds were still not sufficient and for a while it seemed as if William might be on the verge of embarking on another well-intentioned but under-funded failure. Then Claudia, William's daughter, became ill and died on the 5th December. This was a crushing blow. William's first wife and two other daughters were already dead and his second wife had left and returned to Manchester within weeks of the wedding. He never returned to Africa but developed heart disease and went into a sad decline. William could no longer look after himself, nor afford home help. He was reluctantly taken in by a distant relation, Margaret Roberts of 25 New Street, Porthmadoc. His son, Stanley, had declined to look after him and now refused to provide financial support. Margaret Roberts managed to get her local Poor Law Union to offer ten shillings a week for his upkeep but she said she could not really afford to look after him on those terms. This is how the office in Wynnstay Road became involved. In March 1923 the relieving officer, Fred Williams, was wondering how to respond to Ffestiniog Union's request for a payment of fifteen shillings a week. After much to-ing and fro-ing it became clear that nobody really wanted to look after poor William and on 21st December 1923 he was admitted to Conwy Workhouse where he died on 27th January 1924. He now lies buried with other members of his family and five of his African students in the cemetery in Old Colwyn.

7. Continue along Abergele Road towards Old Colwyn. All too frequently a sombre procession, led by a horse-drawn hearse, made its way along this same route as past residents of Congo House travelled to their final resting place: from Kinkasa in 1888 to William in 1924. At the roundabout ascend Llanelian Road for 400 yards and then enter the cemetery, on the left. Head towards a conspicuous stone angel, on your left, quite near the railings, and you should be able to locate each of the following memorials (K), (L), (M) and (N) nearby. There are ten people resting here who are central to the story of Congo House, but some lie together and share memorials.

K. William, his first wife Kate, and his daughters Katie and Edith lie together in a plot marked by a grey stone monument. Little Edith was only six months old when she died on 3rd March 1893. Just over a year later her mother, William's wife, died at the age of thirty-three. Her funeral was attended by all the Great and the Good of Colwyn Bay who were enthusiastic supporters of the Institute in those early years. The hymn Bydd Myrdd o Ryfeddodau was sung here at her graveside. 'Noticeable amongst the floral tributes . . . was a magnificent Welsh harp, with a broken string, from the English Baptist Church, Colwyn Bay.' On 24th May 1909 daughter Katie also passed away, aged twenty-two. She had suffered from chronic rheumatism for seven years and had been bedridden for three years.

L. Claudia, William's longest surviving daughter, lies in a separate grave marked by another grey stone memorial, this time with a trefoil top. Despite her frail health, she was much admired as a gifted teacher and musician. She contracted influenza, which developed into pneumonia and she passed away in the early hours of Monday 5th December 1918, aged 30. Claudia touchingly shares her grave with Ernestina, a black African. One slanderous critic took this to indicate that Ernestina must really have been a bastard daughter of William's adventures in Africa. Ernestina was actually a student placed at the institute by her father who also provided a generous financial settlement for her education. She was not William's daughter by birth but by informal adoption. The Hughes family always treated her as they did their own daughters. When William remarried after his wife's death, Ernestina was there as a bridesmaid along with Katie and Claudia, all wearing 'cream dresses and leghorn hats'. Whilst studying in Colwyn Bay, Ernestina fell in love with a visiting black American missionary, Joseph Morford, who is mentioned on the memorial stone. They were married in Africa and worked together for eight years running a school in Southern Nigeria. They returned to Colwyn Bay in the summer of 1913 for an extended holiday. When Joseph returned, Ernestina intended to stay on for a while but was further delayed by an illness, which proved fatal; she died on January 11th, 1914. A special prayer was recited here at the graveside for her husband, who would not receive the sad news until three more weeks had passed.

M. Four more African students are buried here with graves marked by three sandstone memorials. Kinkasa and Samba share a grave but Kinkasa really belongs with Nkanza. They were William's first pupils. He met them during his first days in Africa in 1882 and found Kinkasa an enthusiastic recruit. Nkanza though, was not only more mischievous but also an indentured slave so William had to give his master a bale of material, worth £4. 10s. before he would allow him to leave. Nkanza was also badly afflicted with 'jiggers' which was rife in the area. This is a parasite, which burrows under the skin and eats the flesh. Nkanza's feet were so badly affected he could hardly stand so William washed his feet and dug out the grubs. This simple act of deep biblical significance greatly impressed Nkanza but in the end it was Kinkasa who won over Nkanza. The two boys nursed William during his severe bout of fever in the Congo and returned with him in 1885 to Wales. They then toured Britain together raising the funds to set up the Institute. Kinkasa sadly died on the 3rd May 1888, aged 15, before Congo House became a reality. Nkanza proved a wonderful student, much admired by all who met him and fondly remembered for his humour and strong Welsh accent. By early 1892 he had achieved excellent academic results and William observed, 'The idea of going home grew in him as he grew and now it is the ardent wish of his heart and burns within him.' Sadly, he didn't make it, he was suddenly taken ill in March and died on Sunday April 3rd 1892, aged sixteen. After a service at Congo House, his coffin was placed into a glass sided horse drawn hearse, followed by six further carriages and many pedestrian mourners who wended their way to his final resting place here. It was a very sad time, coming less than four weeks after the death of Samba who also came from the Congo River area and had also been rescued from slavery. He had been having fun playing on the fields next to Congo House when he fell badly. He seemed fine for a few days but then began to vomit and died from internal injuries on 9th March 1892.

N. Joseph Emmanuel Abraham has another sandstone memorial but it is rather overgrown. He originated from Anaboe on the Gold Coast (Ghana) and was also known by his African name of Kobina Boodoo. He was also a popular and well-known figure in Colwyn Bay and many mourned his death from tuberculosis on 11th April 1909, aged twenty-one. And here our story must end. Congo House was a brave venture and William Hughes a flawed character, but a good man. His detractor, Horatio Bottomley, was an arrogant, xenophobic crook. He won the libel case and even became an M.P. but with dramatic irony he was soon arrested on charges of fraud, found guilty, declared bankrupt, imprisoned for five years and died in poverty.

Bibliography

Baddeley, Richard, *The Borough of Colwyn Handbook* (1987).

Clews, Roy, *To Dream of Freedom* (1980).

Davies, Joan, *Llysfaen: Our Village* (Parts 1-6).

Edwards, Geoffrey, *The Borough of Colwyn Bay* (1984).

Ellis, John Richard, *A History of Abergele and District* (1948).

Emyr, John, *Lewis Valentine yn Cofio* (1983).

Hubbard, Edward, *The Buildings of Wales; Clwyd* (1986).

Hughes, William, *Dark Africa and the Way Out* (1892).

Jones & Rawcliffe, *Llanddulas; Heritage of a Village* (1985).

Large, Frank, *The Liverpool to Holyhead Telegraph* (1998).

Lotz & Pegg, *Essays in Black History 1780-1950* (1986).

Porter, George, *Colwyn Bay Before the Houses Came*.

Roberts, Graham, *Colwyn Bay and District* (3 Vols.).

Rosa Hovey, *Penrhos, 1880-1930* (1930).

Rydal School, *Rydal School 1885-1935* (1935).

Thomas, Dilys, *Old Colwyn from Small Beginnings*.

Tucker, Norman, *Colwyn Bay; Its Origin and Growth*.

Williams, Ellis Wynne, *Abergele; The Story of a Parish* (1968).

Wynne Jones, Ivor, *Colwyn Bay; a brief history* (1995).

Acknowledgements

I would like to thank the following people for their help: Anna Jeffery, Tom Parry, James Berry, R. Helen Phillips, Kathy Roberts, William and Ann Owen, Jean Williams, William Stanley Hughes, Cyril Hughes, Dora Pearson and the staff of the following archives: Denbighshire, Gwynedd, U.C.N.W., Thameside, Merseyside Maritime Museum, and the local history collections of Colwyn Bay and Llandudno Reference Libraries.

Index